CAPODIMONTE

COLLECTIBLES

CONTRIBUTING WRITER

CATHERINE P. BLOOM

PUBLICATIONS INTERNATIONAL, LTD.

CONTRIBUTING WRITER CATHERINE P. BLOOM IS A COLUMNIST FOR *COLLECTORS NEWS* AND
THE GRAND RAPIDS PRESS, AND SHE HAS WRITTEN SEVERAL BOOKS FOR THE COLLECTORS INFORMATION BUREAU.

ACKNOWLEDGMENTS

HANK ADLER, ARNART IMPORTS, NEW YORK, NY 10010,
IMPORTERS AND DISTRIBUTORS FOR "N" CAPODIMONTE CLASSICS.

ANGELO CICCARELLO, EUROPEAN TREASURES COMPANY, CARSON, CA 90746,
EXCLUSIVE IMPORTERS AND DISTRIBUTORS FOR BARBETTA OF FLAVIA PORCELAIN, BENNACCHIO OF TRIADE,
BINDI OF B & M, BORSATO OF ANTONIO BORSATO COMPANY, CAPPÉ OF ROYAL CROWN PORCELAIN,
CAZZOLA OF PORCELLANE PRINCIPE, GALLETTI OF TYCHE, GALLI OF TIZIANO GALLI COMPANY,
MERLI OF KING'S COMPANY, PELLATI OF IPA, PEZZATO OF GINO PEZZATO COMPANY.

ALLEN GOELDNER, NAPOLEON U.S.A., INC., AUDUBON, PA 19407,
IMPORTERS AND DISTRIBUTORS FOR NAPOLEON COLLECTION.

ROBERT HECHT, FOREST LAMPS & GIFTS INC., BROOKLYN, NY 11220,
IMPORTERS AND DISTRIBUTORS FOR LAURENZ CLASSIC COLLECTION BY ENZO ARZENTON.

HERB MILLER, MILLER IMPORT CORPORATION, NEW YORK, NY 10001,
IMPORTERS AND DISTRIBUTORS FOR "THE ARMANI COLLECTION" OF FLORENCE SCULTURE D' ARTE.

DOUGLAS MITCHELL, MUNRO COLLECTIBLES, TOLEDO, OH 43615,
IMPORTERS AND DISTRIBUTORS FOR DEAR SCULTURE ARTISTICHE.

PHOTO CREDITS

THE BRIDGEMAN ART LIBRARY, LONDON: 8; ANGELO CICCARELLO, EUROPEAN TREASURES COMPANY: 187, 188;
MIRCO DECET: 42, 45, 49; SUSAN DIRK, SEATTLE ART MUSEUM: 13, 18;
KAISER-PORZELLAN: 147, 148; PEDICINI, NAPLES: 6, 9-12, 14, 16-25, 27-32, 35;
PORCELLANE RICHARD-GINORI, MILAN: 94, 95.

SAM GRIFFITH PHOTOGRAPHY: ALL OTHER PHOTOS.

FRONT JACKET: "AURORA," BY LUCIANO CAZZOLA FOR PORCELLANE PRINCIPE (SEE PAGE 77).
BACK JACKET, CLOCKWISE FROM TOP: "BOY ON DONKEY," BY LUCIANO CAZZOLA FOR PORCELLANE PRINCIPE
(SEE PAGE 102); "ROYAL OWL," BY VIRGILIO BINDI (SEE PAGE 144);
"OPEN-AIR BREAKFAST," BY GIUSEPPE CAPPÉ FOR ROYAL CROWN PORCELAIN (SEE PAGE 105);
"THE CHEATERS," BY BRUNO MERLI FOR KING'S PORCELAIN (SEE PAGE 47);
DOUBLE-TULIP COLLECTION, "N" CAPODIMONTE COLLECTION, ARNART IMPORTS (SEE PAGE 162).
TITLE PAGE: "PEGASUS," BY AURO BELCARI FOR DEAR SCULTURE ARTISTICHE (SEE PAGE 141).
THIS PAGE AND OPPOSITE PAGE: "HERONS," BY ERMANNO FARINA FOR DEAR SCULTURE ARTISTICHE
(SEE PAGE 142); LILY PLANT, NAPOLEON COLLECTION.

TABLE OF CONTENTS

This perfect rose, hand-crafted in porcelain
by Napoleon Capodimonte Flowers, exemplifies the beautiful
Capodimonte florals being made today.

INTRODUCTION

The very word Capodimonte still evokes passionate admiration in the world's museums and private collections. Although it was produced for less than a century, the original Capodimonte porcelains helped open a new medium of expression and artistic vitality in the wake of the Italian Renaissance. Capodimonte seemed to express the very soul of the Italian experience. The influence of the original Capodimonte has been so profound that it still affects porcelains being produced today.

Ironically, today's Capodimonte is one of the most debated porcelains in the world. Firestorms still erupt when the name Capodimonte is applied to porcelains considered unworthy of the name. This is not a new or academic conflict. It is a struggle that began early in the nineteenth century, when the Capodimonte crown began appearing on porcelains produced in Naples and elsewhere.

No one knows why this practice occurred, but some experts speculate that craftsmen from the original royal Capodimonte factory may have placed the trademark on their own work to indicate their affiliation with the prestigious porcelain works. Others speculate that with no one to protect the authenticity of the royal trademark, the Capodimonte designation was added by unscrupulous porcelain factories strictly for profit. Regardless of original intent, the Capodimonte trademark was adopted by so many porcelain factories in Italy that it became an umbrella term, much like "Staffordshire" or "Dresden" china.

Perhaps part of the appeal of Capodimonte porcelains stems from their romantic past—a past that began with the marriage of a king and a princess. This is a tale of how the princess's dowry triggered a passionate quest for the formula for an Italian porcelain that would attempt to equal the golden age of Italian architecture, sculpture, and art.

THIS FIGURINE OF A YOUNG GIRL CARRYING A BASKET OF BREAD
IS AN EARLY CAPODIMONTE FIGURINE (1745-1755).
HER HEAD IS SMALL IN PROPORTION TO THE REST OF HER BODY,
AND HER FROCK AND APRON ARE QUITE SIMPLE.
SHE STANDS ON THE ROCKY BASE TYPICAL OF EARLY PIECES, BUT HER SLIPPERS
AND THE FLOWERS AT HER FEET REVEAL A GROWING INTEREST IN DETAILING.
GOLD IS USED AS AN ACCENT.
CAPODIMONTE MUSEUM, NAPLES

CAPODIMONTE COLLECTIBLES

THE HISTORY OF CAPODIMONTE

Heavily laden merchant ships returning from ports in Egypt, Syria, and Turkey were the first to bring Chinese porcelain to Italy in the late 1500s.

Italian potters were already producing majolica, which was a biscuit-colored earthenware with an opaque white glaze, and a high-quality glass that could be decorated with enamel. This expertise eventually led to the development of an early soft-paste porcelain. But the first porcelain in Italy wasn't produced until 1720, by Francesco Vezzi, who purchased the secrets from a renegade Meissen workman. A much more successful factory was opened in Doccia by Marchese Carlo Ginori in 1737.

When King Charles VII, a Bourbon, ascended to the throne in 1734 as the King of Naples and the Two Sicilies, he was considered an able leader who admired learning, supported the arts, and was an ardent advocate of the excavation projects at Pompeii and Herculaneum. But his royal wedding in 1738, to Princess Maria Amelia Christina of Saxony, would transform the art of Italian porcelain forever. It was Charles's third marriage, and his new bride was the granddaughter of Augustus the Strong, the founder of the first European porcelain works at Meissen. The 13-year-old bride's dowry included 17 cases of gold-tooled red leather containing 57 sets of table service made of her father's hard-paste Meissen porcelain. Many of these services were decorated with the joint coats of arms of the kingdoms of Saxony and Naples.

CHARLES IS SHOWN IN HUNTING GARB. THIS PORTRAIT BY GOYA Y LUCIENTES WAS PAINTED WHEN CHARLES WAS KING OF SPAIN.
PRADO, MADRID

MARIA AMELIA'S OPULENT RED DRESS MAKES HER LOOK QUITE REGAL, THOUGH SHE WAS CLEARLY NOT A GREAT BEAUTY. THIS PORTRAIT WAS PAINTED BY LOUIS DE SILVESTRE.
PRADO, MADRID

CAPODIMONTE COLLECTIBLES

Struck by the exquisite beauty of the porcelain, Charles immediately began porcelain experiments in the palace courtyard. Most of these early experiments resulted in failure. His workers lacked not only the proper clays and kaolin (a particularly fine, white clay), but also the formulas and expertise needed to produce porcelain. Expeditions were undertaken throughout Italy in search of the proper clays. Charles even sent ships to China in search of elusive clays and other materials needed in making porcelain.

AN IDYLLIC SCENE OF NAPLES AS CHARLES MIGHT HAVE SEEN IT FROM HIS ROYAL PALACE AT CAPODIMONTE, THIS OIL PAINTING, "VIEW OF NAPLES FROM CAPODIMONTE," WAS PAINTED BY ALEXANDRE HYACINTE DUNOUY, WHO LIVED FROM 1757 TO 1843. *CAPODIMONTE MUSEUM, NAPLES*

In spite of these early setbacks, Charles remained optimistic. In 1743 he erected the Royal Manufactory of Porcelain on the grounds of his Royal Palace, which stood on a hill overlooking Naples. It seemed fitting that the name selected for the king's porcelain, Capodimonte, simply meant "top of the mountain."

The following year, the king founded the Accademia del Modello to train young artists and molders for his factory. The factory's chief modeler, Giuseppe Gricci, was named the director of the academy.

A SNUFFBOX DECORATED WITH AN
18TH-CENTURY RENDITION OF
THE OLD TESTAMENT STORY
OF JUDITH, WHO SAVED
THE JEWISH PEOPLE BY
SLIPPING INTO THE TENT OF
HOLOFERNES, THE COMMANDER OF
THE ASSYRIAN ARMY,
AND KILLING HIM.
THE SIDES OF THE BOX ARE
DECORATED WITH MORE TRADITIONAL,
PASTORAL SCENES.
BOTH THE LID AND THE RIM OF THE
BOX ARE ACCENTED WITH GOLD.
MUSEO DUCA DI MARTINA, NAPLES

Thousands of experiments were conducted before the correct ingredients and formulas were discovered, but the king was persistent. Finally, his efforts were rewarded by the development of a soft, white porcelain. The earliest pieces produced with this new material were small, plain white snuffboxes, cane handles, and vases decorated with seashell designs. These designs had a surprisingly clean and elegant appearance, but the influences of the Meissen, Oriental, and French rococo styles were also evident. Gradually, as the formulas for the paste were improved, tea sets, jugs, goblets, coffee and chocolate services, statuettes, and tureens were added to the factory's offerings.

A SMALL SHELL-SHAPED BASIN OR FINGERBOWL FROM THE EARLY CAPODIMONTE PERIOD, ABOUT 1745. NOTICE THE CREAMY WHITE COLOR OF THE PORCELAIN, THE SOFT WAVES IN THE UPPER EDGE, AND THE SEEMINGLY RANDOM PLACEMENT OF SEASHELLS, STARFISH, AND OTHER SEA CREATURES FOR THEIR DECORATIVE EFFECT.
CAPODIMONTE MUSEUM, NAPLES

THIS VERY EARLY (1745-1750) CAPODIMONTE CUP AND SAUCER IS DECORATED WITH PASTORAL SCENES. THE SAUCER SHOWS A GENTLEMAN AND LADY DRESSED IN THE FASHIONS OF THE COURT; THE CUP FEATURES A CHERUB PLAYING SOME SORT OF WOODWIND INSTRUMENT.
MUSEO DUCA DI MARTINA, NAPLES

CAPODIMONTE COLLECTIBLES

TOP, LEFT:
WE CAN ONLY SPECULATE WHY
THE DOG IN THE YOUNG MAN'S ARMS
IS WEARING A BONNET.
BECAUSE OF THE YOUNG MAN'S
SMALL HEAD AND THE STONY BASE
HE STANDS ON, WITH ITS
LEAFLESS STUMP, THIS STATUETTE
IS PROBABLY AN EARLY WORK.
OF SPECIAL NOTE IS THE
MULTICOLORED DECORATIVE DESIGN
USED ON HIS BREECHES.
COLLECTION DE CICCIO,
CAPODIMONTE MUSEUM, NAPLES

TOP, RIGHT:
"THE MILK-WOMAN" IS PROBABLY
AN EARLY FIGURINE.
THE LINES OF HER GOWN ARE
SURPRISINGLY SIMPLE AND ARE
ADORNED WITH TOUCHES OF GOLD,
WITH A BOW ON THE BODICE.
ALTHOUGH THE CONTAINER IN HER
ARMS CONVEY HER DUTIES, HER
FACIAL EXPRESSION GIVES NO
HINT OF HER EMOTIONS.
MUSEO DUCA DI MARTINA, NAPLES

WITH A HUNK OF CHEESE IN ONE HAND AND
A KNIFE IN THE OTHER, "THE CHEESE VENDOR"
LUSTILY HAWKS HIS CHEESE.
THE INTRICATE GOLD PATTERN ON HIS APRON
REVEALS THAT HE IS MORE THAN
AN ORDINARY PEDDLER.
COLLECTION DE CICCIO,
CAPODIMONTE MUSEUM, NAPLES

THIS FIGURINE CAPTURES A LIAISON
BETWEEN A LADY OF THE COURT
IN HER FINERY AND THE YOUNG ARTIST
WHO IS PAINTING HER PORTRAIT—
A PORTRAIT THAT MUST HIGHLIGHT
MILADY'S BEAUTY AND CONCEAL ALL FLAWS.
COLLECTION DE CICCIO,
CAPODIMONTE MUSEUM, NAPLES

"FIGURE OF A YOUTH" WAS PROBABLY PRODUCED BETWEEN 1750 AND 1755.
THE LINES ARE SURPRISINGLY SIMPLE AND UNADORNED,
BUT A GREAT DEAL OF ATTENTION HAS BEEN LAVISHED ON
THE FACIAL EXPRESSION AND SUCH ACCENTS AS
THE GOLD ON THE YOUNG MAN'S DOUBLET.
DOROTHY CONDON FALKNOR COLLECTION OF EUROPEAN CERAMICS,
SEATTLE ART MUSEUM

CAPODIMONTE COLLECTIBLES

TOP, LEFT:
THIS ELEGANT WHITE PORCELAIN
CANDLESTICK IS IN THE
ROCOCO STYLE AND LAVISHLY
DECORATED WITH GOLD.
IT MAY HAVE BEEN USED IN A
CHURCH, BECAUSE THERE APPEARS
TO BE A HAND-PAINTED SCENE
OF THE ASCENSION ON THE BASE.
PRIVATE COLLECTION, NAPLES

TOP, RIGHT:
WHILE THE ROCKY BASE AND
SMALL HEAD HELP TO IDENTIFY
THIS FIGURINE OF A YOUNG GIRL
AMONG THE EARLY CAPODIMONTE
PIECES, HER GRACEFUL GESTURES
AND THE DECORATIVE DESIGNS ON
THE SKIRT SHOW THAT IT WAS
MADE BY AN EXPERIENCED ARTISAN
WHO UNDERSTOOD HOW TO
ACHIEVE THE APPEARANCE OF
GRACEFUL MOVEMENTS.
*COLLECTION DE CICCIO,
CAPODIMONTE MUSEUM, NAPLES*

BOTTOM, LEFT AND RIGHT:
VENDORS LIKE THE MAN WITH A
BASKET OF RING-SHAPED CAKES (LEFT)
AND THE WOMAN SELLING STATUETTES
(RIGHT) WERE COMMON SIGHTS,
HAWKING THEIR WARES
IN THE STREETS OF NAPLES.
THEIR DISPROPORTIONATELY
SMALL HEADS ARE TYPICAL OF
EARLY (1745-1750) CAPODIMONTE
FIGURINES. THE SCULPTOR
HAS CAPTURED THE SHIFTS IN
POSTURE NEEDED TO CARRY
HEAVY BASKETS ALL DAY.
A DEFT TOUCH HAS BEEN USED
TO CREATE THE DESIGNS ON THE
SKIRT AND BREECHES.
CAPODIMONTE MUSEUM, NAPLES

Tradition holds that Charles was allergic to the flowers in the palace's gardens, and that the entire genre of exquisitely fashioned roses and other blossoms were created so that the king could enjoy perfect ceramic and porcelain blossoms without suffering the discomforts of constant sneezing and weeping eyes.

The earliest Capodimonte pieces had no markings. When a trademark was introduced, Charles selected the fleur-de-lis in honor of his Bourbon lineage. The impressed fleur-de-lis was placed within a circle. The painted fleur-de-lis, which varied in thickness, was freestanding and was usually done in gold or blue. Toward the end of Charles's reign, the fleur-de-lis was sometimes replaced by a double C.

PROUD OF HIS BOURBON HERITAGE, CHARLES USED A FINELY LINED FLEUR-DE-LIS ON HIS EARLIER PIECES.

The formula for a hard-paste porcelain eluded Charles's chemists until 1785. In the intervening years, at least four totally different kinds of mixed pastes were employed: one greenish-gray, one yellow, and two imperfect white pastes. The fine, white translucent paste that was finally developed was greatly enhanced with the use of a clean, clear glaze, which gave the colors a new brilliance. Many of the early works were quite small or even miniatures, but the development of more suitable mediums allowed for larger, more ambitious pieces. Many of these works have survived because they were given to other monarchs as gifts of state.

Folklore says that Charles took an active role in the experimentation and even tried his hand at a potter's wheel. When he was away at war, Charles demanded monthly reports from the factory. He also was on hand for the annual fair in front of the palace, where the first porcelains were sold. Later, he frequented the small shop in the center of town where his porcelains were displayed and sold. It was rumored that a large purchase was a sure passport to the king's favor.

Meticulous records of these sales were preserved, and today they provide art historians with an invaluable tool in identifying these early porcelains. The factory's records also reveal the working conditions—the 12- to 14-hour workdays—and an account of the stiff prison sentence imposed on an artist convicted of stealing the decorative gold dust entrusted to his care.

In 1745, the king appointed Tuscan chemist Giovanni Remici as director of coloring and gilding and Giuseppe Gricci as chief modeler. It was Remici who created the famous Capodimonte shades of brown, green, purple-pink, and orange-red.

Gricci modeled many of the factory's masterpieces, such as the "Madonna della Pieta," but the everyday life in Naples Bay was also very evident in Gricci's art. He introduced the use of branches of coral and other marine motifs, which gradually evolved from simple marine decorations to finely detailed figurines of fishermen holding baskets of fishes and other bounty. The old *commedia dell'arte,* the popular itinerant theatre, also provided Gricci with great inspiration. One of his most popular series contained individual figures and groups of figures from the Italian *commedia.*

Formed on a stylized rock base, Gricci's figures were distinguished by their easy fluid movements and small heads. Contrary to common belief, the figurines had an uncluttered look and were not in the rococo tradition.

ALTHOUGH THIS SMALL DUCK ON A WHITE BASE SEEMS CRUDE BY TODAY'S STANDARDS, ITS VITALITY AND BEARING MAKE IT AN INTERESTING EXAMPLE OF THE CAPODIMONTE FACTORY'S EARLY ATTEMPTS AT REALISTIC BIRD AND ANIMAL SCULPTURES. *COLLECTION DE CICCIO, CAPODIMONTE MUSEUM, NAPLES*

IN THIS MULTI-FIGURED FIGURINE, A YOUNG MAN OFFERS A CUBE OF SUGAR TO A SMALL DOG IN THE ARMS OF ITS YOUNG MISTRESS. ALTHOUGH THE PIECE IS NOT DATED, IT CLEARLY REPRESENTS A LATER PERIOD OF CAPODIMONTE. THE ROUGH STONE BASE REMAINS, BUT THE COMPOSITION OF THE PIECE IS MORE SOPHISTICATED, THE DETAILING IS MORE EXACTING, AND A MUCH WIDER SPECTRUM OF COLORS HAS BEEN USED TO ACHIEVE THE DECORATIVE DESIGNS.
COLLECTION DE CICCIO, CAPODIMONTE MUSEUM, NAPLES

THE FIGURINE OF A SMALL GREEN BIRD ON A BRANCH IS ONE OF THE EARLIEST EXAMPLES OF CAPODIMONTE BIRD FIGURES. ALTHOUGH UNPRETENTIOUS, THE DETAILING OF THE BEAK AND THE EYES SEPARATE THIS FIGURINE FROM OTHER FIGURES OF THE PERIOD.
COLLECTION DE CICCIO, CAPODIMONTE MUSEUM, NAPLES

CAPODIMONTE COLLECTIBLES

TOP:
"THE DRUMMER BOY" (1745-1750)
IS A VERY EARLY EXAMPLE OF
CAPODIMONTE FIGURINES.
THOUGH THE PORCELAIN HAS AN
OFF-WHITE COLOR, THIS FIGURINE
SHOWS A SURPRISING VITALITY
AND ATTENTION TO DETAILING.
NOTICE THE CARE WITH WHICH
THE CAPE IS DRAPED OVER THE
BOY'S SHOULDER.
CAPODIMONTE MUSEUM, NAPLES

BOTTOM, LEFT:
A VERY EARLY (1750-1755) BEAKER
DECORATED WITH AN ALL-GREEN
FIGURE OF A MAN WITH A BOOK OR
HYMNAL IN ONE HAND AND A
BELL IN THE OTHER.
THE SYMBOLISM OF THIS ALMOST
ORIENTAL-LOOKING FIGURE
IS UNCLEAR.
DOROTHY CONDON FALKNOR COLLECTION
OF EUROPEAN CERAMICS,
SEATTLE ART MUSEUM

BOTTOM, RIGHT:
THIS EARLY FIGURINE (1748-1752)
CAPTURES THE INTENSE EMOTIONS
OF AN ACTOR DEEPLY ENGROSSED
IN HIS CRAFT, WHILE HIS
FAITHFUL DOG LOOKS ON.
THE ACTOR'S MOVEMENTS SEEM
MORE LIFELIKE THAN THOSE IN
SOME EARLY FIGURES, AND
THE DECORATIVE DESIGN ON HIS
DOUBLET AND BREECHES REVEALS
AN ATTENTION TO COSTUMING.
COLLECTION DE CICCIO,
CAPODIMONTE MUSEUM, NAPLES

TOP:
THIS SMALL MULTICOLORED GROUP FIGURINE SHOWS AN OLD SEAMSTRESS, WHO NEEDS TO WEAR SPECTACLES, EXPLAINING THE INTRICACIES OF FINE EMBROIDERY STITCHES TO A YOUNG GIRL. NOTICE THE DELICATE DECORATIVE PATTERNS ON THE GIRL'S SKIRT AND THE INTRICATE BORDER DESIGN ON THE HEM OF THE TEACHER'S GOWN.
COLLECTION DE CICCIO, CAPODIMONTE MUSEUM, NAPLES

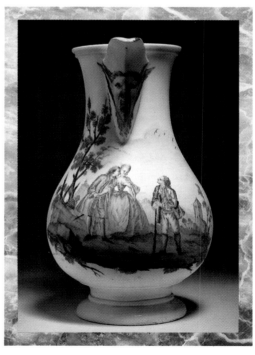

BOTTOM, LEFT:
"THE GREENGROCER" (1748-1752) HAS THE SMALL HEAD TYPICAL OF THE EARLY FIGURINES. EACH OF THE VEGETABLES HE IS SELLING SEEMS TO HAVE BEEN INDIVIDUALLY FASHIONED. ALTHOUGH THE PALETTE OF COLORS USED IN DECORATING THESE FIGURINES IS SOMEWHAT LIMITED, THE BOY'S STRIPED BREECHES, DECORATED VEST, AND BUCKLED SHOES REFLECT A GROWING ATTENTION TO CLOTHING.
CAPODIMONTE MUSEUM, NAPLES

BOTTOM, RIGHT:
MADE IN THE TRADITIONAL SHAPE, THIS EARLY (1750) CAPODIMONTE COFFEEPOT IS DECORATED WITH A GARDEN SCENE.
A GENTLEMAN OF THE COURT WHISPERS SWEET NOTHINGS INTO MILADY'S EAR WHILE ANOTHER GENTLEMAN LOOKS ON.
A MYTHICAL IMAGE DECORATES THE SPOUT OF THE POT.
MUSEO DUCA DI MARTINA, NAPLES

CAPODIMONTE COLLECTIBLES

A CLOSE VIEW OF TWO OF THE CHINESE MANDARIN
FIGURES IN THE PORCELAIN ROOM AT PORTICI
SHOWS THE FACIAL EXPRESSIONS ACHIEVED
BY THE USE OF BAS-RELIEF FIGURES.
THE INTRICATE BAS-RELIEF BASKET FILLED WITH
APPLES FORMS A STRIKING CONTRAST WITH
THE FLAT PASTORAL BACKGROUND.
A SMALL TREE IS ACCENTED WITH LEAVES,
BIRDS, AND EVEN BUTTERFLIES.
THE RICHLY PATTERNED ROBES OF THE FIGURES
CAPTURE BOTH THE BEAUTY AND CUSTOMS
OF THE CHINESE CULTURE.
CAPODIMONTE MUSEUM, NAPLES

OPPOSITE PAGE:
THE PORCELAIN ROOM AT
CHARLES'S PALACE AT PORTICI
WAS CONSTRUCTED BETWEEN
1757 AND 1759.
ITS THOUSANDS OF PORCELAIN
PANELS ARE DECORATED WITH
MANDARIN FIGURES, VINES,
AND FLOWERS.
CAPODIMONTE MUSEUM, NAPLES

In 1757, King Charles gave his staff a most extravagant commission. They were to begin work on a gift for the young queen, a *salottino di porcellana* (room of porcelain) at Portici, their summer palace. Introduced at the Bourbon Court in France, these elegant rooms of porcelain were completely decorated with porcelain and were considered the ultimate decor. Though the room at Portici was considered small by royal standards, its ceiling, walls, and floor were made entirely of panels of porcelain and mirrors. More than 3,000 interlocking white porcelain panels overlaid with colored porcelain reliefs were needed at Portici. Decorated in the Chinese mode, the room incorporated elements of mandarin figures and elegant Chinese landscapes, rococo styling, and bas-relief flowers, fruits, and garlands. An elaborate porcelain chandelier encrusted with porcelain birds and flowers was suspended from the ceiling.

THE LINED FLEUR-DE-LIS WAS
GRADUALLY ENLARGED AND
WIDENED DURING CHARLES'S TIME
AT BUEN RETIRO.
THIS SYMBOL WAS USUALLY
IN GOLD OR BLUE.

Unfortunately, the royal couple never really had a chance to fully enjoy the beauty of their *salottino di porcellana*. In 1759, Charles VII succeeded to the throne of Spain as Charles III. Unwilling to abandon his interest in porcelain, Charles took the entire factory with him. When he set sail from Naples, his retinue included more than 40 of his workmen, molders, and modelers. The factory's molds and four tons of porcelain paste were also aboard. Ironically, everything that was left behind was then destroyed so that the Capodimonte reputation would remain intact.

One of Charles's first priorities in his new kingdom was to build a new porcelain factory, Buen Retiro, in Madrid. The early porcelains produced at Buen Retiro are difficult to distinguish from the earlier Capodimonte pieces because the same materials and craftsmen were employed. Very little Spanish influence was apparent during this period. Gricci continued as chief modeler, and the descendants of Ottavio Schepers, a chemist and the factory's chief technician, continued to supervise production. There were a few disputes with local Spanish workmen and a feud of sorts gradually developed between the Schepers and Gricci families, but members of both families continued to work at Buen Retiro until the end of the century, when they died or retired.

A short time after Charles arrived in Spain, he commissioned two new porcelain rooms. One was at Aranjuez and the other was at the Royal Palace in Madrid. Although they were considered more ornate and ambitious, they were never totally completed and have not received the attention of the room at Portici.

Experimentation continued in the search for a true hard paste, but most of the factory's production was for the ornamentation of the king's palaces. Without the stimulation of trade or contact with the outside world, the vitality of the porcelain factory began to ebb.

TYPICAL OF THE EARLY CAPODIMONTE DINNERWARE, THIS SET IS DECORATED WITH COBALT BLUE AND GOLD. THE SUGAR BOWL, PLATE, CUP, AND SAUCER ARE PAINTED WITH A SIMPLE PASTORAL SCENE WITH A GREAT HOUSE IN THE BACKGROUND. A PORCELAIN SHELL FORMS THE KNOB ON THE LID OF THE SUGAR BOWL.
MUSEO DUCA DE MARTINA, NAPLES

In 1788, Charles attempted to generate needed funds by selling porcelains, but few were purchased. A few months later, he died and was succeeded on the throne by his son Charles IV. The factory continued to operate with inexperienced workmen, and the supplies of clay that Charles brought from Italy were finally exhausted. Eventually, the Buen Retiro factory was producing figurines of an inferior soft paste that were decorated in garish colors in an unsuccessful attempt to resemble the late-18th-century Staffordshire figures in England.

Eager to restore his father's reputation for high-quality porcelain, Charles IV sent D. Bartolome Sureda to France to learn the processes used in the porcelain works at Sèvres. On his return, Sureda was appointed director of the factory and immediately started work on the formula for a new paste. A short time later, he developed a paste that could be subjected to high temperatures without harm and that was said to be even superior to the biscuit ware at Sèvres. Dinner services were then produced on a grand scale in an attempt to compete in the world market.

Unfortunately, the Sureda regime was cut short in 1790 by an invasion of French troops, who dealt a death blow to the factory. The buildings were turned into a fortress. The looting by the foreign troops was followed by an uprising of Spanish patriots, who in their fury destroyed everything. But it was the British military forces who totally destroyed the Buen Retiro factory in 1812.

THIS FORMAL PORTRAIT OF FERDINAND IV BY ANTON RAPHAEL MENGS IS CROWDED
WITH TANTALIZING HINTS OF THE YOUNG KING'S ROYAL PRIVILEGE.
THE MARBLE BACKGROUND, THE GILDED TABLE AND CHAIR, ALONG WITH HIS CAPE
OF RED VELVET TRIMMED WITH ERMINE AND HIS CROWN REVEAL HIS WEALTH AND STATUS.
CAPODIMONTE MUSEUM, NAPLES

CAPODIMONTE COLLECTIBLES

FERDINAND IV

When Charles set sail with his retinue for Spain in 1760, he left behind his eight-year-old son, Ferdinand IV, on the throne of Naples and the Two Sicilies.

The magnificent porcelain room in the palace at Portici must have been a constant reminder of his father's ambition. When young King Ferdinand IV came of age in 1771, one of his first tasks was to reestablish his father's porcelain factory. A master builder was engaged to construct a factory in the park of the Villa Portici, and a handful of the original Capodimonte workers were urged to return. The factory marks for the Portici factory were painted in blue and included a crown, a capital R, 1772, and a small wave.

Almost from the beginning, the newly constructed building was considered too small for the enterprise. The builder was again engaged, this time to convert an old building near the Royal Palace in Naples. By 1773, the new factory was producing items in the modified rococo style and appearance of the early Capodimonte period. Made with a very glassy, translucent soft paste and covered by a glaze with a soft yellow color, the pieces were clearly reminiscent of his father's earlier efforts. Marked pieces from this period bear the monogram F.R.F. *(Fabbrica Reale Ferdinandea)* surmounted by a crown painted in blue, red, or sometimes black enamel. Later, the more traditional crown with a capital N underneath painted in blue became the factory mark.

AN IDEALIZED SCENE BY 18TH-CENTURY ARTIST G. MALADARELLI COMMEMORATES CHARLES III TRANSFERRING THE REGENCY OF NAPLES TO HIS SON FERDINAND IV, SEATED AT THE TABLE. *CASERTA, PALAZZO REALE*

THE BLUE TRADEMARK OF
FABBRICA REAL FERDINANDEA
FEATURED A CROWN AND
THE LETTER N.
A NUMBER OF SIMILAR SYMBOLS
WERE ALSO USED BY
THE GINORI FACTORY.

Although the artistic influence of Meissen is unmistakable, the pieces produced in Ferdinand's factory also reveal the influences reminiscent of Chantilly or Vincennes, rather than the German prototypes. A frequent design included small bunches of flowers, usually incorporating a rose in full bloom surrounded by wildflowers, all richly painted in naturalistic colors and arranged in an asymmetrical grouping. Landscapes and views with people also appear, clearly influenced by contemporary native painters and engravers. A stippled style, achieved by using large brushes to fill in the contours, was replaced in the late 1770s by a miniature technique used to decorate coffee and tea sets. These compositions frequently depicted young suitors or cupids seated on clouds and had a rococo mood. However, the borders of the plates and saucers were decorated with motifs that are more neoclassical than rococo in spirit. The continued success of the excavations at Pompeii and Herculaneum helped to initiate a revival of the classical decorative style.

The sculptural work of this first period of the Royal Ferdinand Factory retains the exaggerated movement and the small heads characteristic of Gricci's models, but the bases are quite different. Instead of the stylized rocky mound that Gricci favored, these figures stood on a round, smooth mound with a richly embellished C scrolled in relief.

In 1780, Domenico Venuti was promoted to director of Ferdinand's factory. Under his leadership, the factory grew in importance, and artists were encouraged to adopt the neoclassical style.

Ferdinand repeated his father's laborious search for a better-quality porcelain that would not be subject to cracks and flaws produced in the firing. The rather creamy-colored paste developed during this period was ideal for the many neoclassical wares then being produced.

THE EXTENSIVE FAMILY OF FERDINAND IV,
ALONG WITH THEIR PETS AND PASTIMES,
APPEAR AGAINST A TYPICALLY
PASTORAL BACKGROUND IN THIS FORMAL
FAMILY PORTRAIT BY 18TH-CENTURY
ARTIST ANGELICA KAUFFMAN.
CAPODIMONTE MUSEUM, NAPLES

A PLATE AND BEAKER DECORATED
WITH THE HARBOR AND THE VOLCANO
NEAR POMPEII.
IT WAS THE EXCAVATIONS BY BOTH
CHARLES AND FERDINAND AT POMPEII
THAT LED TO THE INTRODUCTION
OF THE HIGHLY STYLIZED
CLASSICAL DESIGNS LIKE THE
PATTERN ON THE RIM OF
THIS PLATE.
PRIVATE COLLECTION

THIS TÊTE-À-TÊTE SERVICE WITH RED
NEOCLASSICAL FIGURES WAS PRODUCED AROUND
1790 DURING FERDINAND'S REIGN.
THIS SERVICE INTEGRATES ALL
THE ELEMENTS OF THE NEOCLASSICAL REVIVAL.
THE DECORATION SHOWS ANCIENT FIGURES OF
GREEK AND ROMAN MYTHOLOGY
WITH THE SYMMETRICAL BORDERS OF
AN EARLIER CLASSICAL PERIOD.
CAPODIMONTE MUSEUM, NAPLES

CAPODIMONTE COLLECTIBLES

THIS FIGURINE OF A MOTHER AND CHILD REPRESENTS A REAL BREAKTHROUGH FOR FERDINAND'S SCULPTORS. THE FACIAL EXPRESSIONS ON THESE SIMPLE PEASANT FOLK ARE SOFT, AND THEY SEEM TO EXPRESS SUCH REAL EMOTIONS AS LOVE AND CONCERN. THE DRAPE OF THE MOTHER'S APRON AND THE DESIGN ON THE HEM OF HER SKIRT REVEAL THE ARTIST'S GROWING DECORATIVE SKILLS. EVEN THOUGH THE WOMAN'S FEET REST ON DIRT AND STONE, THE BASE IS PAINTED AND FINISHED WITH A DECORATIVE DESIGN.
COLLECTION DE CICCIO, CAPODIMONTE MUSEUM, NAPLES

PRODUCED DURING THE REIGN OF
FERDINAND, THIS AMPHORA VASE
HAS HANDLES IN THE SHAPE OF
SMALL SATYRS AND IS DECORATED
WITH A PORTRAIT OF FERDINAND IV.
ALTHOUGH THE ROYAL PROFILE
MAY HAVE FLATTERED THE KING,
IT IS NOT AS INTRIGUING AS THE
DELICATE DECORATIVE DESIGNS
IN GOLD THAT COVER MOST
OF THE VASE.
COLLECTION DE CICCIO,
CAPODIMONTE MUSEUM, NAPLES

CAPODIMONTE COLLECTIBLES

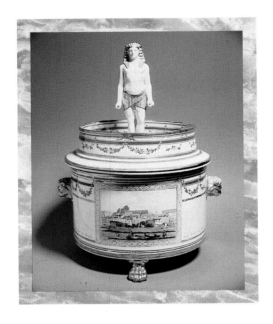

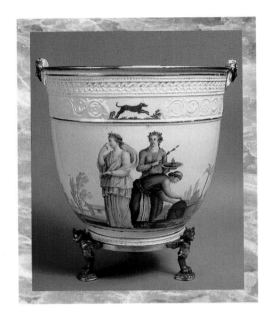

THIS ICE CREAM BOWL PRODUCED DURING FERDINAND'S
REIGN IS DECORATED WITH A CITY SURROUNDED BY
A NEOCLASSICAL BORDER. NOTICE THE GOLD CLAW FEET
AND THE LION'S-HEAD HANDLES.
A FIGURE OF AN EGYPTIAN TOPS THE LID, WHICH IS
FESTOONED WITH GARLANDS OF FLOWERS AND
RED AND BLUE RIBBONS.
CAPODIMONTE MUSEUM, NAPLES

A HERCULANEAN SERVICE COOLER FROM
THE ROYAL FACTORY (1780-1782)
IS MOUNTED ON A BRONZE BASE AND DECORATED WITH
MYTHOLOGICAL FIGURES.
THE PORCELAIN APPEARS TO BE MUCH FINER
WITH A PURER WHITE COLOR.
NOTICE THE USE OF HUMAN HEADS AS HANDLES.
PRIVATE COLLECTION, NAPLES

A PAIR OF CACHEPOTS PRODUCED IN
THE ROYAL FACTORY DURING FERDINAND'S REIGN.
THE QUALITY AND COLOR OF THE PORCELAIN IS
IMPROVED, AND GOLD NEOCLASSICAL BORDERS NOW
DECORATE THE RIM AND THE PAINTING EDGES.
THE HANDLES ON BOTH POTS ARE CLASSICAL FACES.
COLLECTION DE CICCIO,
CAPODIMONTE MUSEUM, NAPLES

THIS TEAPOT AND SUGAR BOWL REFLECT THE
GROWING INTEREST IN NEOCLASSICAL THEMES.
THE TEAPOT SHOWS THE ERUPTION OF THE NEARBY
VOLCANO AT POMPEII; THE SUGAR BOWL SHOWS
A CLASSICAL LYRE PLAYER. THE PIECES ARE
DECORATED IN GOLD CLASSICAL DESIGNS.
A GOLDEN, REGAL TIGER CROUCHES ON EACH LID.
MUSEO DUCA DE MARTINA, NAPLES

THIS FIGURINE, "THE GALLANT COUPLE," WAS PRODUCED IN
FERDINAND'S ROYAL FACTORY BETWEEN 1784 AND 1788.
ALTHOUGH THE ROUGH STONE BASE THAT WAS USED
IN THE EARLIEST FIGURINES IS STILL EVIDENT, HERE
IT HAS BEEN MOLDED AND PAINTED
TO RESEMBLE GRASS.
PRIVATE COLLECTION, NAPLES

CAPODIMONTE COLLECTIBLES

AN EXAMPLE OF A GROUPING ON A BENCH
OF FIGURES CONTEMPORARY TO
FERDINAND IV. DRAWN TOWARD
THE ACTIVITIES OF THE NEWLY EMERGING
BOURGEOISIE, FERDINAND FOUND THEIR
SIMPLE PLEASURES A CHARMING SUBJECT
FOR A NEW GENRE OF FIGURINES.
THE ARTIST HAS ATTEMPTED TO CAPTURE THE
MANNERS AND FASHIONS OF THE DAY.
COLLECTION DE CICCIO,
CAPODIMONTE MUSEUM, NAPLES

A COVERED SOUP TUREEN AND TRAY
PRODUCED DURING FERDINAND'S REIGN.
THE HAND-PAINTED SCENES
DECORATING BOTH PIECES WERE
BASED ON TRADITIONAL DEPICTIONS
OF THE NEAPOLITAN HARBOR AND
THE CITY ON ITS BANKS.
IN ADDITION TO THE SMALLER
NEOCLASSICAL BORDER AROUND THE
PAINTING ON THE TRAY,
THE WIDE YELLOW RIM WITH DECORATIVE
PATTERNS HAS BEEN INTRODUCED.
THE MYTHOLOGICAL ANIMAL USED ON
THE LID OF THE TUREEN ALSO
REFLECTS THE NEOCLASSICAL MODE.
COLLECTION DE CICCIO,
CAPODIMONTE MUSEUM, NAPLES

THE JOYS OF PARENTHOOD ARE HIGHLIGHTED
IN THIS CHARMING GROUPING OF FIGURES
PRODUCED IN THE ROYAL FACTORY DURING
FERDINAND'S REIGN. THE ELEGANCE OF
THE LADY'S GOWN AND CHAPEAU REVEAL THE
IMPORTANCE OF FINERY IN SOCIAL LIFE.
THE JOVIAL AND EXPANSIVE NATURE OF THE
GENTLEMAN IS CONVEYED BY HIS GOLD BUTTONS
AND THE RUFFLES AND BOWS OF HIS SHIRT.
THEIR BLOND CHILD COMPLETES THIS GROUPING.
COLLECTION DE CICCIO,
CAPODIMONTE MUSEUM, NAPLES

In 1781, the factory undertook one of its most important commissions, a major Etruscan table service based on the latest discoveries at the Herculaneum site. Commissioned as a gift for Ferdinand's father, Charles III of Spain, the centerpiece was a bisque sculpture representing Charles and his son continuing the excavations, surrounded by reproductions of the latest finds. A second service of 282 pieces was made as a diplomatic gift for George III of England and was delivered in 1787. A large part of this set, known as the Etruscan Service, can still be seen at Windsor Castle, but the centerpiece, representing Tarchon, King of the Etruscans, attending a gladiators' match, is now lost. It was decorated with figures done in red or black, imitating the style of ancient Greeks.

Other services produced during this period have borders embossed with arabesque patterns or grotesques and painted with designs from antiquity. Topographical views of the Kingdom of the Two Sicilies, especially of Naples, were also used to decorate the ware.

The figurines and sculptural groups produced between 1790 and 1800 clearly reflect the life of the court of Ferdinand IV. Ferdinand's interests were not the cultural interests of his father, Charles; he enjoyed hunting, fishing, and buffoonery. At court, he was surrounded by members of the bourgeoisie. Ferdinand's modelers delighted in producing figurines that revealed not only the rich clothing and ornaments of the bourgeoisie, but also their pretentious manners and attitudes, which made them appear strangely plebeian.

The most pleasing pieces of these small decorative figures show three or four men and women seated on a bench in a garden. Each figure is wearing the latest fashions. Occasionally a figure may be accompanied by a small child or dog. These miniature compositions were realistically modeled and made in a brilliant porcelain, delicately painted to show even the patterns on the dresses. They provided a vivid impression of nouveaux-riches families enjoying their outings. A few of these groups were made in biscuit ware, but their lack of color and glazing make them less lively.

Early in 1799, the French entered Naples and, as a result of a popular uprising, the Parthenopean Republic was proclaimed. Ferdinand IV fled under the protection of the British fleet to Palermo, where he remained for about six months. When the republic failed, he returned to Naples and took severe reprisal against the leaders of the rebellion. Ferdinand IV did not resume his interest in porcelain, and without his patronage the factory plunged into debt.

Napoleon's activities produced a political scene that was unsettling. Undecorated porcelain began arriving from France to be painted, and the items produced by the factory adopted the current French styles. Clocks and candlesticks were frequently decorated with the Egyptian motifs associated with the Napoleonic period.

In 1803, Napoleon proclaimed himself the President of the Italian Republic. The following year, his brother, Joseph Bonaparte, was made King of Naples. Joseph had no interest in being the patron of porcelain art, and in 1807, he sold the Naples factory to the French firm Jean Poulard & Co. It proved to be a poor arrangement, and numerous lawsuits ensued. Around 1807, the manufacturing of colored or decorated porcelain ceased. Only a fragmented and curtailed production of biscuit ware continued until the factory completely collapsed around 1817. Ferdinand had been restored to the throne after the defeat of Napoleon in 1815, but his interest in porcelain had disappeared. The molds and models were sold to the Ginori factory of Doccia sometime between 1834 and 1840, although there is some question about the date.

The Golden Age of Capodimonte had come to an end.

BASED ON THE GREEK MYTH OF EUROPA, A PHOENICIAN PRINCESS WHO WAS ABDUCTED
TO CRETE BY ZEUS IN THE GUISE OF A WHITE BULL, THIS "PORTRAIT OF EUROPA"
RECREATES ONE OF THE FIRST "BEAUTY AND THE BEAST" MYTHS.
NOTICE HOW THE GARLANDS OF FLOWERS ARE INTERTWINED AROUND THE FIGURES
OF EUROPA, THE BULL, AND THE SMALL CHERUBS OR *PUTTI.*
CAPODIMONTE MUSEUM, NAPLES

CAPODIMONTE COLLECTIBLES

"ONCE UPON A TIME..." ("C'ERA UNA VOLTA...") WAS SCULPTED BY
LUCIANO CAZZOLA FOR PORCELLANE PRINCIPE IN 1988.
IT IS A LIMITED EDITION OF 500.
THIS IS A SUPERB EXAMPLE OF A MULTI-FIGURED
SCULPTURE DONE IN PASTORAL STYLE.
SET IN A COUNTRY KITCHEN, THE SCENE SHOWS THE WHITE-HAIRED GENTLEMAN
TELLING A STORY TO THE LITTLE GIRL.
NOTICE THE TILT OF HER HEAD AND THE QUIZZICAL EXPRESSION ON HER FACE.
IN THE BACKGROUND, THE AMUSED MOTHER CONTINUES TO PREPARE SUPPER
WHILE ENJOYING THE STORYTELLER AND HIS RAPT LISTENER.

CAPODIMONTE
TODAY

This could have been the end of the Capodimonte story, but it wasn't. The rich legacy of fine porcelain remained as vivid reminders of the genius that had been nurtured by Capodimonte. The modelers and artisans who had played such important roles returned to their homes and to the thousands of small porcelain works throughout the countryside. Much like seeds blown to earth, the modelers' images and the molders' formulas and techniques were buried throughout Italy. To the world, it appeared that the glory that once surrounded Capodimonte had completely disappeared. The Ginori factory at Doccia continued to produce porcelain figurines using the Capodimonte molds on a limited basis, but it is generally accepted that the traditional style had become overworked and uninspired.

In 1896, the factory of Ginori merged with the Milanese factory Richard and the factory name Richard-Ginori was created. After World War II, the old factory at Doccia was rebuilt in Seso Florentino, where the Doccia Museum was established. As a preeminent producer of porcelain, Richard-Ginori still retains the Capodimonte tradition of high-quality porcelain and elegant hand-painting.

Elsewhere, the first real stirrings in the rebirth of the Capodimonte traditions appeared in 1925, when Signora Carozzi, a gifted lady who had been inspired by the ancient masters of the Capodimonte tradition, founded the Industria Lombardo Porcellane Artistiche (ILPA). While the traditions of the Capodimonte art form were respected, copying the old masterpieces was discouraged. Instead, the young artists who flocked to ILPA were challenged to discover for themselves, much as the artists at Capodimonte had done before them. Although ILPA played a pivotal role in the renaissance of the Capodimonte art form, it was simply the spark that was then snuffed out.

ILPA was disbanded, but from this now-forgotten porcelain factory a new, more famous company, IPA (Industria Porcellane Artistiche), emerged. IPA was committed to uncompromising standards. Formulas for new porcelains were discovered, and artists and sculptors created not only the ornate and romantic traditional court figures, but also figures that revealed the vitality and complexity of the everyday life of the Italian people.

Though the courtly figures remained ornate, the figures and groupings of peasants and the working class were stripped clean of ornamentation. Instead, facial expressions and body movements revealed a detailed realism that captured life's pathos and its humor.

IPA survived the turmoil of World War II with its reputation among connoisseurs intact. Artists Giorgio Pellate, Guiseppe Cappé, Alessandro Tosca, and Sandro Maggioni were among the most important artists to work for IPA during the post-war period.

Many of IPA's artists remained within the family, but in 1952, a talented group of artists—Cappé, Redaelli, and Merli—broke away from IPA and formed King's Porcelain. Although the King's Porcelain trademark is still in use as a symbol on respected works, both Cappé and Merli eventually went on to establish their own studios. Cappé's work is now produced by Royal Crown Porcelains and Merli established his own studio in 1960. His works are marked with the name "B. Merli." Another artist to break with IPA was Sandro Maggioni. One of IPA's finest artists, Sandro later established his own Elite factory.

GIUSEPPE CAPPÉ WAS THE CHIEF SCULPTOR AT IPA BEFORE MOVING TO KING'S PORCELAIN. THE PORCELAIN FIGURE "ORGAN GRINDER" WAS PRODUCED WHILE HE WAS AT KING'S. ALTHOUGH CAPPÉ NEVER HESITATES TO INCLUDE HOMELY DETAILS, HE TREATS THEM WITH SUCH RESPECT AND GENTLENESS THAT WE GROW TO LOVE THEM.

BOTTOM, LEFT: "THE PIANIST" IS BY GEORGIO PELLATI, A MEMBER OF THE NEW GENERATION OF SCULPTORS AT IPA. THE ECCENTRIC PIANIST HAS DISLODGED THE IVORY OF ONE KEY SO THAT IT CURLS UPWARD.

BOTTOM, RIGHT: PELLATI OF IPA CREATES BITING SATIRICAL SCULPTURES MUCH LIKE THE FIGURINES PRODUCED BY EARLY CAPODIMONTE ARTISANS. "THE ATTORNEY" MOCKS THE FOIBLES OF THE LEGAL PROFESSION. THE LAWYER'S BLACK AND PURPLE ROBES CANNOT CONCEAL HIS SOUR DISPOSITION OR THE PAUNCH ACQUIRED BY EATING TOO WELL.

THE BEAUTY OF "LA FLORA," THE GODDESS OF FLOWERS IN ROMAN MYTHOLOGY, IS CAPTURED BY GIOVANNI BARBETTA IN THIS ORNATE FIGURINE FOR FLAVIA CERAMICHE PORCELLANE. SHE IS PORTRAYED AS A SLENDER YOUNG MAIDEN DRESSED IN A FLOWING GOWN AND CROWNED WITH A GARLAND OF FLOWERS. FLORA AND A PAIR OF *PUTTI* (LITTLE CHERUBS) STAND ATOP A FOOTED PORCELAIN BASE GILDED WITH GOLD AND DECORATED WITH ROSEBUDS AND ANOTHER SMALL *PUTTO*.

In 1975, an important new porcelain factory, Porcellane Principe, was founded. Here a new generation of artists, modelers, and painters who were trained in the best modern techniques employed their skills in the old Neapolitan school of Capodimonte. To further strengthen their ties to prestigious Italian factories with roots that go back to the Naples of 1800, Porcellane Principe recently purchased the classical Mollica factory. At Principe, three men—Sergio Traforetti, Lino Gobbi, and Luciano Cazzola—have combined their talents to bring new life to the ancient Capodimonte tradition.

"A GRAPE FOR TWO," BY GIOVANNI BARBETTA FOR FLAVIA CERAMICHE PORCELLANE, IS AN ELEGANT STUDY IN THE ADAPTATION OF THE PASTORAL GENRE FOR MORE MODERN TASTES. RELAXING ON THE GRASS, A YOUNG SHEPHERD AND SHEPHERDESS AMUSE THEMSELVES BY EATING GRAPES. TRADITIONALLY STYLED, BOTH ARE HANDSOME AND THEIR CLOTHING HUMBLE WITH A ROMANTIC PERFECTION.

Artist Giovanni Bresolin, known as Barbetta, is a skillful, capable sculptor whose work is currently associated with the Flavia of Marsan. He has created a number of porcelain lines such as "Linea Classica." The colors, influenced by the Sèvres and Saxony traditions, are softer and warmer than those of many Capodimonte pieces. There is an order and sense of serenity about Barbetta's figures of young girls with agile adolescent bodies clothed with garments that barely seem to touch the skin.

With these artists, the Capodimonte tradition continues.

ONE OF THE MAIN PIAZZAS IN BASSANO DEL GRAPPA IS PIAZZA LIBERTÀ,
BESIDE THE CHURCH OF ST. JOHN.
THE CHURCH DATES FROM THE 14TH CENTURY.

A TOWN THAT
MAKES PORCELAIN

Most Capodimonte today is not made in Naples, but in the north of Italy. Nestled in the shadow of Mount Grappa, a landmark in the Dolomite Mountains of Italy, is the small city of Bassano del Grappa, which is a center for making porcelain objects. A gateway to the spectacular scenery of Italy's northern mountain region, Bassano del Grappa is on the Brenta River, which begins as a stream fed by the mountains' snow. After wending its way through Bassano del Grappa, the river travels on to Padua before finally making its way into the lagoons of Venice.

Bassano del Grappa is a typical Italian city, with a population of about 30,000. Many of the buildings are old and are gradually being renovated by a new generation that has come to appreciate their beauty. The city has some very pretty sections, and in the center of town there are streets lined with shops selling the locally produced porcelains.

Blessed with a natural reserve of high-quality, pure white clay, Bassano del Grappa inevitably became a center for porcelain and ceramic production. Local pottery works benefited greatly when the royal porcelain factories were closed and the skilled artisans returned to towns and villages like Bassano del Grappa. Unwilling to relinquish the techniques they had learned, many of these sculptors and artisans began producing their own lines of porcelain. These small family-owned factories nurtured the porcelain industry, and the ancient techniques were handed down from generation to generation.

In Bassano del Grappa today, there are about 250 porcelain factories of various sizes. Many of them are small family businesses. They make figurines, flower pots, and accessories for sale to shops, where tourists can buy a memento from their Italian holiday, and for export to the United States, to Canada, and to other countries. In addition to the local porcelain shops, cooperatives and company representatives handle orders for porcelain from all over the world.

Some families in Bassano del Grappa have been working in porcelain for three or four generations or more. In these family-owned businesses, any adult members of the family who take an interest and have an aptitude for porcelain-making may take part. One family member may be an expert in the firing process, and another may handle the design work. Because a steady hand is needed for painting and decorating, young adults are frequently employed as painters. By law, children under the age of 14 are not allowed to work, but a local art school has a specialized course of study in the art of making porcelain.

Marriages and separations frequently alter family relationships. After centuries of these changing alliances, the loosely knit structure of an Italian family seems to be little affected. It is not considered unusual for a person to leave one family factory and join another. And since the making of porcelain is difficult, laborious work, many individuals choose to work in other occupations instead of joining their relations in a porcelain factory. For this reason, workers are recruited from elsewhere in Italy and also from such places as Tunisia and Algeria.

Gradually, many of the factories began to specialize in one specific item. Some make flowerpots; others specialize in florals, figurines, or tableware. A family's decision to specialize was determined in part by an individual's taste, education, and skill. A factory blessed with a sculptor

AGAINST THE BACKDROP OF THE DOLOMITES,
THE BRENTA RIVER IS SPANNED
BY THE PONTE DEGLI ALPI,
AN OLD WOODEN BRIDGE THAT WAS THE SITE
OF FIERCE FIGHTING DURING WORLD WAR I.

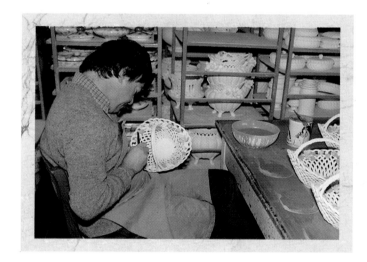

THIS MAN IS PAINTING CERAMIC BASKETS
AT RIGONI AND SONS, A FIRM RUN
BY A BROTHER AND SISTER.
THEY SPECIALIZE IN DECORATIVE
ACCESSORIES AND ART OBJECTS FOR EXPORT.

THE FIRM OF RAZZETTI, WHERE THIS WOMAN
IS WORKING ON CHANDELIERS,
HAS BEEN PRODUCING CAPODIMONTE
FOR THREE GENERATIONS.

CAPODIMONTE COLLECTIBLES

capable of producing elegant human figurines may find that the talents of the next generation are more suited to making flowerpots.

In recent years, a number of large porcelain manufacturers have opened factories in Bassano del Grappa to take advantage of the abundant supply of clay and a work force familiar with the porcelain process. These large manufacturers have designers who develop ideas for porcelain pieces. At the present time, the designs from these firms dominate the field. Their new lines developed for the corporate porcelain companies are widely copied.

An artist at a large porcelain factory will design a piece, which is then shown to the dealer who will sell the piece. The customer critiques it, and it is returned to the design department, which oversees any modifications. The piece is then produced according to the dealer's specifications. Once the piece is completed, it is offered for sale in a shop or in another marketing venue.

A sharp-eyed buyer may purchase this new item, take it to one of the smaller porcelain factories, and ask the factory to work up a similar item at a lower cost. The factory will work around the clock to produce the replication, and they are sold at a cheaper price.

A patent or copyright on a distinctive design can be obtained, but it is a very expensive and time-consuming process. If a piece were to be modified during the course of production, the patent would not apply to the modified version. As a consequence, most designs are not patented. Even among major manufacturers, common themes and patterns occur.

Because of the pride and affection the Italians have for their traditions, many of today's porcelains are modifications of earlier themes. Figurines dressed in the costumes of the royal court have always been popular with collectors, as have figurines that evoke a pastoral setting.

A NUMBER OF CAPODIMONTE LINES
CARRY A MODEL SHOWING
A GROUP OF CARD PLAYERS
IN WHICH ONE OF THE GROUP
PASSES A CARD UNDER THE TABLE
WITH HIS TOES.
"THE CHEATERS," BY BRUNO MERLI
FOR KING'S PORCELAIN,
SHOWS FOUR ANIMATED YOUNG
BOYS WHOSE FACIAL EXPRESSIONS
REVEAL THEIR GOOD HUMOR.
THE AGILE CUNNING OF THE YOUNG
GAMBLER TRANSFERRING A CARD
WITH HIS FOOT INSPIRES
THE BOY AT THE OTHER END OF
THE TABLE TO GIVE US
A HORRIFIED LOOK.

IN "THE FOUR CHEATERS," BY
ENZO ARZENTON FOR THE
LAURENZ CLASSIC COLLECTION,
THE THEME IS INTERPRETED
DIFFERENTLY. ARZENTON HAS
REPLACED TWO OF THE BOYS
WITH SEASONED GAMBLERS.
IN ADDITION, EACH OF THE FOUR
PLAYERS IS PASSING A CARD
THAT IS WORTHLESS TO HIS
OWN HAND BUT FILLS OUT
THE HAND OF THE PLAYER
ON HIS RIGHT.

CAPODIMONTE COLLECTIBLES

However, major importers sometimes request designs on a particular theme that will appeal to the collectors they sell to. For that reason, a porcelain manufacturer may produce an item that is not based in the Italian tradition.

To some experts, only pieces in a style that carries on the tradition begun by King Charles can be called Capodimonte. The definition of "true Capodimonte" is difficult to arrive at. Some manufacturers believe that they are carrying on the tradition that began with King Charles. Others are quick to say that, although they work in the Capodimonte style, the true Capodimonte was produced only by King Charles's factory, and today it can be seen only in museums and private collections.

Several experts believe that high-quality Capodimonte art is being produced today, but only in porcelain; the many objects being produced in softer materials or in a newer technology cannot be classified as true Capodimonte. Many figurines are now made in a new material called "cold-cast porcelain," which hardens naturally without being fired in a kiln. Other experts on collectibles say that none of the arts has remained untouched by time, and it would be a mistake to dismiss works that employ modern materials and technology. Ultimately, choosing any collectible piece is a personal choice. Each piece must be judged on its design and craftsmanship.

Most Capodimonte models carry the blue crown and N that is typically associated with Capodimonte, usually in addition to a backstamp, factory mark, or name. But the crown and N are not fully protected, and the name Capodimonte can now indicate "the style of Capodimonte." A careful collector buys models only from the best factories and looks for the backstamp that indicates the figurine's real origin.

On Via Angarano, just off the Ponte degli Alpi, this shop sells porcelain and ceramics to visitors to the town.

Bassano del Grappa is lavishly dotted with small shops that sell figurines and decorative items. This shop is also near the Ponte degli Alpi.

Most of the eminent Capodimonte sculptors are in northern Italy not far from Bassano del Grappa. Napoleon Flowers are made in Brescia; Antonio Borsato's studio is in Milan; Porcellane Principe is in Vicenza; Florence Sculture d'Arte is in Siena.

CAPODIMONTE COLLECTIBLES

"MOTHER ON A GARDEN SEAT," SCULPTED BY LUCIANO CAZZOLA
FOR PORCELLANE PRINCIPE, IS A TOUCHING EXAMPLE OF A MOTHER'S LOVE.
DRESSED FOR THE ROYAL COURT IN A FULL SKIRT DECORATED WITH ROSEBUDS,
THE YOUNG MOTHER'S ATTENTION IS FOCUSED, NOT ON HER ATTIRE,
BUT ON THE INFANT IN HER ARMS.
THE IDYLLIC ILLUSION IS ENHANCED BY THE FLOWERS
AT MILADY'S SIDE.

CAPODIMONTE COLLECTIBLES

HUMAN FIGURINES

The richness and diversity of today's Capodimonte figurines reflect the Italian artisans' rich cultural heritage. Although the gift for creating realistic human figures was developed by Greek sculptors, Roman sculptors soon surpassed their Greek rivals, and the human figure became the quintessential subject of art during the Italian Renaissance. An enlightened Bourbon monarch, King Charles was a product of both the French and Italian cultures. Although the first objects produced in King Charles's porcelain factory were trinkets such as snuffboxes, cane handles, and saucers, there is little doubt that Charles envisioned porcelain figures that would equal the human sculptures of his countrymen.

Charles's efforts were impeded because, as one of the first porcelain makers in Italy, he had no means of obtaining the essential trade secrets needed to produce fine porcelain. In spite of this seemingly insurmountable obstacle, his master modeler Gricci soon began producing crude figures with small heads and a surprising vitality and energy.

Two types of figurines were produced during this early period. Inspiration for the highly colored statuettes and figurines was drawn from court life and Naples's cosmopolitan waterfront—a mecca for ships from all the known world. The quasi-comic seamen and fishmongers who inhabited the Neapolitan docks and the buffoons and clowns of the *commedia dell'arte* provided a wealth of fresh inspiration.

Other, somewhat smaller figures drawn from mythological sources and the idyllic pastoral pleasures of royalty adorned vases and bowls. The flat surfaces of all kinds of vessels soon became the backdrops for pastoral sketches and for figures molded in low relief and delicately colored.

Perhaps the most characteristic pieces produced at Naples were the little detached figures, which were generally grotesques that were delicately modeled and painted. Because the secrets of the pure white glazes still eluded Capodimonte artisans, porcelains from the earlier periods have a pleasant warm color.

Later, during the reign of Charles's son Ferdinand IV, the classical and mythological themes gave way, and figurines were based on the newly emerging middle class—the bourgeoisie whose values Ferdinand admired.

When the Royal Capodimonte factory was closed in the early 1800s, the artisans were cut off from the royalty and the urban bourgeoisie. Working in small porcelain factories scattered throughout the countryside, they shifted their attention to the everyday life of the country folk. These lighthearted glimpses of rural pleasures soon became so popular that at times they threatened to overshadow the earlier courtly figures.

Like their predecessors, today's artists and sculptors clearly depend upon the world around them for inspiration. The touching relationship between mother and child is as pleasing a subject as the innocence and vivacity of children at play. Clowns, with their painted smiles and ill-fitting clothes, are also a popular theme. Ballerinas forever poised *en pointe* continue to charm collectors. And the Capodimonte tradition of illustrating the work of tradesmen and professionals has continued uninterrupted.

Themes used by the early artists of Capodimonte are still favorites of today's collectors. Figurines produced by modern studios include old favorites such as goddesses in flowing gowns, dwarflike grotesques, and coquettish ladies with hooped skirts and powdered hair. Shepherd boys still guard their flocks, and young maidens fill their baskets with freshly plucked flowers.

ANTONIO BORSATO'S
TRADEMARK.

A CHILD'S TRIP TO THE BARBER
CAN BE AN OPPORTUNITY TO SHARE A COMMON EVENT WITH ADULTS.
THIS SUBDUED YOUNG BOY LOOKS AS IF THE HAIRCUT
WAS SOMEONE ELSE'S IDEA.
A MASTER OF REALISM, ANTONIO BORSATO HAS FITTED HIS "BARBER"
WITH THE TOOLS OF THE TRADE.
NOTICE THE PILE OF MINUTE PORCELAIN HAIR CLIPPINGS
THAT HAVE BEEN SWEPT UP UNDER THE BROOM.

CAPODIMONTE COLLECTIBLES

"THE ANTIQUARIAN," BY LUCIANO CAZZOLA,
IS ONE OF THE FINEST EXAMPLES OF THE CURRENT CAPODIMONTE ART.
ALTHOUGH THIS IS AN UNUSUALLY LARGE PIECE, IT CONTAINS ONLY TWO FIGURINES.
A BEAUTIFUL YOUNG WOMAN HAS COME TO SELL HER JEWELRY,
AND THE ANTIQUARIAN EXAMINES HER SET OF PEARLS.
BUT IT IS THE ANTIQUARIAN'S SURROUNDINGS THAT PIQUE OUR REAL INTEREST.
THE WINDOWS ARE BROKEN, THE CURTAINS ARE HUNG HAPHAZARDLY,
THE FLOOR IS LITTERED WITH PAPER, AND OBJECTS OF ART AND MEMORABILIA
ARE DISPLAYED EVERYWHERE. THIS MUSEUM-QUALITY PIECE
IS PRODUCED BY PORCELLANE PRINCIPE IN A LIMITED EDITION OF 500.

THE ANTIQUARIAN EVALUATES THE YOUNG WOMAN'S PEARLS WITH A PRACTICED EYE.
THE YOUNG WOMAN, WHO IS ATTEMPTING TO NEGOTIATE A BETTER PRICE FOR HER PEARLS,
IS JUST UNCLASPING HER GOLD BRACELET.
PERHAPS SHE IS THINKING OF ADDING THE BRACELET TO THE SALE.
THOUSANDS OF INTRICATE DETAILS HAVE BEEN WOVEN INTO THIS WORK OF ART.
THE ANTIQUARIAN'S ROOM IS FURNISHED WITH AN UNUSUAL MIXTURE OF OBJECTS OF ART
AND EVERYDAY CLUTTER, GIVING THE ROOM AN UNEXPECTED RICHNESS.
EACH OF THESE SCULPTURES IS INDIVIDUALLY PRODUCED,
SO THAT DETAILS MAY VARY FROM PIECE TO PIECE.

CAPODIMONTE COLLECTIBLES

THE TRADEMARK FOR TYCHE.

"MATERNITY," BY GALLETI OF TYCHE, IS AN UNUSUAL FAMILY GROUPING
OF A MOTHER AND TWO CHILDREN.
DRESSED IN A FULL-LENGTH GOWN FROM AN EARLIER PERIOD,
THE MOTHER IS HOLDING A YOUNG BOY ON HER LAP
AS HER DAUGHTER SITS BESIDE HER ON A SETTEE.
WHILE THE MOTHER'S EXPRESSION IS RESERVED, HER DAUGHTER
SEEMS TO BE ENJOYING HER YOUNGER BROTHER.

"SUMMER FUN," CREATED BY GIORGIO PELLATI FOR IPA,
IS A PERFECT EXAMPLE OF TODAY'S PASTORAL CAPODIMONTE.
THE YOUNG LOVERS ENJOY A SWING AMID A PLEASANT OUTDOOR SETTING.
THE THICK ROOTS AND STURDY BRANCH OF THE TREE OFFER A SHARP CONTRAST
TO THE INNOCENT YOUTHFULNESS OF THE COUPLE.

"PLAY TIME," BY ANTONIO BORSATO, IS AN EXTREMELY ATTRACTIVE FIGURINE
OF A YOUNG MOTHER ENJOYING HER CHILDREN.
WHILE HOLDING ONE CHILD IN HER ARMS, SHE SMILES DOWN ON ANOTHER YOUNG CHILD,
WHO IS ENTREATING HER TO LIFT HIM OUT OF HIS WALKER.
IN THIS WORK, BORSATO HAS CAPTURED THE SIMPLE JOYS
EXPERIENCED BY MOTHERS AND CHILDREN.

In "Rock-a-Bye," sculpted by Luciano Cazzola for Porcellane Principe,
the image of a mother rocking and feeding her baby
becomes a touching moment.
The radiant beauty of the young woman is balanced
by the rich drape of her skirt and
the more traditional designs on the base of the figurine.

CAPODIMONTE COLLECTIBLES

59

GINO PEZZATO'S "SERENADE WITH MANDOLIN" RECREATES A YOUNG SUITOR'S ATTEMPT TO WIN A YOUNG LADY'S HEART BY PLAYING LOVE SONGS ON THE MANDOLIN. FROM THE EXPRESSION ON HER FACE, HE HAS AT LEAST GAINED HER ATTENTION.

GINO PEZZATO'S TRADEMARK.

"ALPINE BOY AND GIRL," BY PEZZATO, SHOWS FINE DETAILING IN THE FEATHER IN HIS CAP AND THE FLOWERS AT THEIR FEET.

PEZZATO CAPTURES THE LIGHTHEARTED SPIRIT OF CHILDHOOD IN "LAUNDRY GIRL." THE WIND WHIPS THE HAIR AND SKIRT OF A YOUNG PEASANT GIRL.

"FIRST BATH," BY PEZZATO,
RECALLS AN EARLIER TIME
WHEN BATHS WERE AN
OUTDOOR EVENT.
WHILE A PAIR OF WHITE DOVES
WATCHES THE PROCEDURE
FROM A NEARBY FENCEPOST,
A YOUNG GIRL WITH SOAP
AND TOWEL SEEMS TO BE
TAKING CHARGE OF THE EVENT.
THE COMBINATION OF A NUMBER
OF ELEMENTS IN THIS FIGURINE
MAKES THIS A
VERY HAPPY PIECE.

"MAIL BOY" IS A FINE EXAMPLE OF
THE GENTLE APPEAL OF PEZZATO'S CHILDREN.
NO ONE COULD REFUSE TO ACCEPT
A LETTER FROM THIS CHERUBIC MESSENGER.

THIS SPIRITED BOY IS THE "WINTER"
FIGURINE FROM
PEZZATO'S "FOUR SEASONS"
SERIES.

CAPODIMONTE COLLECTIBLES

THE ART OF THE BALLET IS
KNOWN FOR ITS
PRECISION AND GRACE.
IN "BALLETTO FLY" FOR
KING'S PORCELAIN,
ANTONIO MARINO HAS CAPTURED
A CLIMACTIC MOMENT
IN WHICH THE BALLERINA
BENDS TOWARD THE FLOOR,
WHILE HER PARTNER BOTH
SUPPORTS HER AND JOINS HER
IN HER GRACEFUL
DOWNWARD MOTION.

"FLIGHT OF ANGEL," BY GIUSEPPE CAPPÉ
FOR ROYAL CROWN PORCELAIN,
REVEALS THE SCULPTOR'S TOTAL COMMAND
OF HIS MEDIUM.
HE EMPLOYS A TRADITIONAL
ARABESQUE POSITION, BUT RATHER
THAN THE TUTU, HE HAS CHOSEN
A SIMPLE SKIRT FOR THE BALLERINA.
HER POSE IS COMPLICATED BY THE RIBBON
IN HER OUTSTRETCHED WRIST.
IN CONTRAST TO THE FIGURE, CAPPÉ
HAS CHOSEN A BASE EMBOSSED WITH GOLD.

IN HIS "BALLET CLASS,"
ANTONIO BORSATO HAS CREATED
A SELF-CONTAINED STAGE
ON WHICH THE DANCERS,
MUSICIANS, AND BALLET MASTER
PLAY OUT THEIR ASSIGNED ROLES.
AGAINST THE CREAMY WALLS
AND ARCHES AND REFLECTED BY
THE MIRROR, ONE OF
THE BALLERINAS PRACTICES
AT THE BAR WHILE A PAIR OF
DANCERS EXECUTES A TRADITIONAL
ARABESQUE POSITION.

IN HIS "BALLETTO POSE,"
ANTONIO MARINO SHOWS
THE *PAS DE DEUX*.
THE EXQUISITELY FORMED DANCERS
APPEAR TO BE SUSPENDED
IN TIME AND SPACE.
NOTICE THE CAREFUL ATTENTION TO
THE FACIAL EXPRESSIONS AND
THE BALLERINA'S TUTU.

C A P O D I M O N T E   C O L L E C T I B L E S

IT TAKES MORE THAN
OUTRAGEOUS CLOTHING TO
MAKE A CLOWN.
IN ANTONIO BORSATO'S FIGURINE
"PAGLIACCI,"
THE SCULPTOR HAS ADDED
EXAGGERATED BEHAVIOR
AND MOVEMENTS.
FROM THE TUFTS OF HIS HAIR
TO THE POINTS OF HIS
ELONGATED SHOES, THE CLOWN WITH
THE SAXOPHONE APPEARS A
RIDICULOUS CREATURE,
AND WE LAUGH AS HIS COMPANION
RAISES AN ARM AS IF TO
STRIKE HIM
OR URGE HIM ON.

THIS YOUNG AND EXTREMELY
APPEALING CLOWN IS FROM THE
ARMANI COLLECTION BY
GIUSEPPE ARMANI.
FILLED WITH DREAMS OF LAUGHTER
AND GOOD TIMES, THE
DISAPPOINTMENTS OF LIFE
HAVE NOT YET LEFT THEIR MARK
ON HIS FACE AND FIGURE.
THIS FINELY DETAILED FIGURINE IS
MADE OF COLD-CAST PORCELAIN.

PITY THE POOR CENSUS TAKER
WHO STUMBLES UPON
THE WOMAN WHO
"HAD SO MANY CHILDREN
SHE DIDN'T KNOW WHAT TO DO."
IN THIS FIGURINE, "CENSUS,"
TIZIANO GALLI'S WRY HUMOR
SURFACES AS THE
CENSUS TAKER ATTEMPTS
TO OBTAIN AN
ACCURATE COUNT
OF THE PEOPLE LIVING IN
THE WOMAN'S HOUSEHOLD.

SENSITIVITY AND GOOD HUMOR
ARE APPARENT IN THE
"BOW TIE CLOWN," SCULPTED BY
AURO BELCARI IN COLD-CAST PORCELAIN
FOR THE DEAR CLOWN SERIES.
DESPITE THE EXAGGERATED EYE MAKEUP
AND PAINTED SMILE,
THE CLOWN'S HUMANITY SEEMS
TO SHINE THROUGH.
NOTICE THE SHARP POINT OF HIS HAT
AND HIS MORE-THAN-AMPLE
STRIPED BOW TIE.

THIS MINIATURE BUST OF
AN OLD MAN IS LESS
THAN THREE INCHES TALL.
IT IS PART OF A SERIES
OF BUSTS THAT GINO
PEZZATO HAS SCULPTED
THAT DEPICT DIFFERENT
TYPES OF OLD MEN.

"THE DOCTOR," FROM ROYAL CROWN PORCELAIN, IS AN EXAMPLE OF
THE GENTLE HUMOR OF GIUSEPPE CAPPÉ.
A CHARLIE CHAPLIN–LIKE CHARACTER IS SITTING ON A PARK BENCH.
THERE IS A LOOK OF APPREHENSION ON HIS FACE AS HE LISTENS CAREFULLY THROUGH HIS
STETHOSCOPE TO HIS OWN HEARTBEAT.

THIS SMALL FIGURINE OF
LUDWIG VAN BEETHOVEN,
BY GINO PEZZATO, IS SIMILAR
IN MANY WAYS TO THE
GROTESQUES THAT WERE
PRODUCED DURING THE VERY EARLY
CAPODIMONTE PERIOD.
THIS NEW SERIES OF FAMOUS
COMPOSERS CURRENTLY CONTAINS
18 FIGURES.

"CLOWN WITH SAXOPHONE," SCULPTED BY GIORGIO PELLATI FOR IPA,
IS A SUBDUED, ALMOST PENSIVE WORK.
ALTHOUGH THE PAINTED FACE, THE SMALL HAT,
AND THE COSTUME MAY EVOKE LAUGHTER,
THE CLOWN'S HUMANITY AND QUIET CONCENTRATION ON HIS INSTRUMENT
MAKE HIM A SYMPATHETIC CHARACTER.

CAPODIMONTE COLLECTIBLES

ALTHOUGH SCULPTOR TIZIANO
GALLI IS BETTER KNOWN FOR
HIS UNIQUE, OFTEN SATIRICAL
STYLE, THERE IS NO MALICE
IN HIS FIGURINE
"THE TAILOR."
GALLI CAPTURES THE TAILOR'S
STOOPED SHOULDERS, THE
FOLDS OF HIS SHIRT,
AND HIS SLENDER FINGERS.
AS IN MUCH ITALIAN ART,
THIS FIGURINE SHOWS A BOUQUET
OF HAND-FASHIONED ROSES.

ON THE TAILOR'S TABLE ARE REALISTIC,
DETAILED TOOLS OF THE
TAILOR'S TRADE—AN IRON, SCISSORS,
AND TINY BUTTONS.

TIZIANO GALLI HAS BREATHED
NEW LIFE INTO THE OLD
FAIRY TALE OF "CINDERELLA"
("CENERENTOLA").
THE ELEGANT COSTUMES OF
THE ROYAL COURT
REVEAL THE SPLENDOR OF BOTH
PRINCE CHARMING AND
CINDERELLA.
THE PRINCE IS ON HIS KNEES
IN FRONT OF CINDERELLA,
THUS CONFIRMING THE
OVERWHELMING POWER OF
A GREAT BEAUTY.
FINELY DETAILED IN PORCELAIN,
THIS IS A GOOD EXAMPLE OF
THE CAPODIMONTE ART.

"LADY WALKING," BY LUCIANO CAZZOLA
FOR PORCELLANE PRINCIPE,
WAS CREATED SPECIFICALLY FOR
THE AMERICAN CAPODIMONTE MARKET.
THE LADY'S TRIM FIGURE AND
GRACEFUL MOVEMENTS ARE
HIGHLIGHTED BY A COLORFUL GOWN
AND DECORATED PETTICOAT.
AT HER FEET, TINY FLOWERS ADD
A NATURAL BEAUTY TO HER WALK.

CAPODIMONTE COLLECTIBLES

"WINSTON WITH DRUM" WAS SCULPTED BY AURO BELCARI FOR DEAR'S CLASSIC SERIES. A COLD-CAST PORCELAIN FIGURINE, IT SHOWS A YOUNG BOY LOOKING UP AT HIS AUDIENCE WHILE BEATING ON THE SMALL DRUM BETWEEN HIS LEGS. ALTHOUGH HIS CLOTHING IS NEAT AND WELL CARED FOR, HIS BARE FEET GIVE THE IMPRESSION THAT HE LIVES ON SOME TROPICAL ISLAND WHERE THERE IS NO NEED TO PROTECT FEET FROM INCLEMENT WEATHER.

THE "INDIAN MAIDEN,"
SCULPTED BY MARCELLO
SALVESTRINI FOR DEAR,
IS AN EXCEPTIONALLY
ATTRACTIVE PIECE OF WORK.
PRODUCED OF COLD-CAST
PORCELAIN, IT IS A HIGHLY
ROMANTIC PIECE EVOKING
THE AMERICAN WEST.
THE ARTIST'S RESTRAINT
IN CREATING THE HAIRSTYLE
AND THE BUCKSKIN DRESS
ADDS TO THE AUTHENTICITY
OF THIS FIGURINE.

CAPODIMONTE COLLECTIBLES

GIUSEPPE CAPPÉ HAS CAPTURED THE COUNTENANCE OF AN AGING NEPTUNE,
KING OF THE SEA, IN THIS FIGURINE FOR ROYAL CROWN PORCELAIN.
ALTHOUGH HIS WHITE HAIR IS THINNING AND HIS BROW IS LINED,
HE REMAINS IN COMMAND OF HIS REALM.
RELAXING ASTRIDE HIS THRONE
EMBELLISHED WITH CREATURES FROM THE DEEP,
NEPTUNE HOLDS A TRIDENT IN HIS HAND.
THE SILVER-COLORED DECORATIONS ARE OVERLAYS OF PLATINUM.

CLASSICAL FIGURES

Myths are frequently described as the realities of the spirit. These old tales of the valor and deceit of the gods have been told and retold for centuries. While the power of the gods of Roman mythology has gradually diminished, their influence is still felt in the world of art. It was the physical beauty and perfection of the gods and goddesses that first attracted artists. But the fundamental tests of character shared by both gods and humans have provided artists with tantalizing inspirations.

A brooding and aging Neptune, god of the sea, holds his traditional trident and intently views his realm. The beguiling goddess Aurora, responsible for the daily journey of the sun across the sky, handles her spirited horses and chariot with the skill and grace only goddesses can achieve.

Many of the mythological pieces are accented by small cherublike creatures called *putti,* which attend the gods in Italian Renaissance paintings. The figurines representing Poetry and Music are each receiving inspiration from a chubby, winged *putto.*

Figures of Bacchus, god of grape-growing and riotous living, show both the humor and debauchery of the gods. In many pieces, the elegant godlike figure of Bacchus is attended by handmaidens bearing goblets of wine and playing lutes. Their frenzied poses leave no doubt of the revelry. The *putti* add an innocent note to the scene.

IN "CHILDREN," GIUSSEPE CAPPÉ HAS SCULPTED A LOVABLE PAIR OF *PUTTI* ENGAGED IN PLAY. PRODUCED BY ROYAL CROWN PORCELAIN, CAPPÉ'S *PUTTI* ENABLE US TO SUSPEND REALITY AND ACCEPT THIS PLAYFUL PAIR AS IF THEY WERE SIMPLY CHILDREN.

GIUSEPPE CAPPÉ RECREATES
ALL THE MOST CHARMING
QUALITIES OF THE GODS IN
"THE POETRY" FOR
ROYAL CROWN PORCELAIN.
PORTRAYED AS A HANDSOME
YOUNG MAN, POETRY IS
CLAD IN FLOWING SCARLET
ROBES AND HOLDS A QUILL
IN ONE HAND AND A BOOK
IN THE OTHER.
A *PUTTO* HOVERS NEARBY TO
CAPTURE EVERY WORD
FROM THE MUSE'S LIPS.

CAPODIMONTE COLLECTIBLES

"THE MUSIC," BY CAPPÉ FOR
ROYAL CROWN PORCELAIN,
IS A COMPANION PIECE
TO "THE POETRY,"
AND IT IS ALSO CLASSICAL
IN COMPOSITION AND
IN COSTUME.
MUSIC IS SHOWN AS
A BEAUTIFUL YOUNG WOMAN
PLAYING A LYRE, WHILE A
PUTTO ACCOMPANIES HER
ON THE FLUTE.

CAPODIMONTE COLLECTIBLES

75

IN "THE GLADIATORS," ONE OF THE GLADIATORS HAS FALLEN,
WHILE HIS COMPANION CONTINUES TO WIELD HIS SWORD
IN MORTAL COMBAT WITH A LION.
THE ARTIST, TIZIANO GALLI,
HAS CREATED AN ANIMATED WORK OF ART,
WHICH SHOWS THAT THE OUTCOME IS YET TO BE DECIDED.

CAPODIMONTE COLLECTIBLES

LUCIANO CAZZOLA HAS INTERPRETED "AURORA" FOR PORCELLANE PRINCIPE.
IN THIS CLASSIC WORK, AURORA IS SEEN RIDING HER CHARIOT ACROSS THE SKY.
CAZZOLA HAS MADE THE PAIR OF WHITE STALLIONS LARGE AND ANIMATED,
WHEREAS AURORA'S CHARIOT APPEARS SMALL.
ALTHOUGH HER FIGURE SEEMS FRAGILE,
THERE IS NO QUESTION THAT SHE CONTROLS THE DAY'S JOURNEY.

CAPODIMONTE COLLECTIBLES

IN HIS "TRIUMPH OF BACCHUS" FOR ROYAL CROWN PORCELAIN,
GIUSEPPE CAPPÉ SHOWS A TYPICAL IMAGE OF BACCHUS.
THE GOD OF HARVEST AND REVELRY,
BACCHUS IS PORTRAYED AS A FUN-LOVING GOD WHO ENJOYS
THE COMPANIONSHIP OF YOUNG BEAUTIES AND
THE PLEASURES OF A GOBLET OF WINE.

THE *PUTTI* AT THE FEET OF THE GOD
ADD AN INNOCENT, CHERUBIC
NOTE TO THE REVELRY.

TRULY A SCULPTURE IN THE ROUND, "TRIUMPH OF BACCHUS"
HAS A COMPOSITION AND STRUCTURE
THAT IS GRACEFUL WHEN VIEWED FROM ALL SIDES:

CAPODIMONTE COLLECTIBLES

BRUNO MERLI'S "AURORA," DEPICTING THE ANCIENT MYTH
OF THE GODDESS OF LIGHT, IS PRODUCED BY KING'S PORCELAIN.
EACH MORNING, AURORA BEGINS HER JOURNEY ACROSS THE SKY TO BRING LIGHT TO THE WORLD.
TWO SPIRITED WHITE HORSES PULL HER GOLDEN CHARIOT
WHILE A PAIR OF CHERUBS—ONE BEARING A TORCH AND ANOTHER
HOLDING A GOLDEN DRAPERY—ACCOMPANY HER ON HER WAY.

CAPODIMONTE COLLECTIBLES

GIUSEPPE CAPPÉ HAS A RARE GIFT FOR ENDOWING MYTHOLOGICAL FIGURES
WITH COMELY HUMAN ATTRIBUTES.
"DIANA," THE GODDESS OF THE HUNT,
IS A FAIR-HAIRED YOUNG WOMAN ATTIRED IN A TUNIC OF SOFT PURPLE.
SHE HOLDS THE BOW AND ARROWS NEEDED TO JOIN THE HUNT.

CAPODIMONTE COLLECTIBLES

THIS FINELY DETAILED "MADONNA,"
BY AURO BELCARI FOR DEAR,
HAS AN ANTIQUE,
ALMOST MEDIEVAL APPEARANCE.
HER LONG, FLOWING
RED GOWN SEEMS TO SHIFT
WITH HER MOVEMENTS, AND
HER TRADITIONAL BLUE ROBE
RESTS EASILY ON
HER SHOULDERS.
MADE OF COLD-CAST PORCELAIN,
THIS FIGURINE RETAINS
THE FINE DETAILS AND BEAUTY
THAT CAN ONLY BE OBTAINED
WITH HAND-PAINTING.

CAPODIMONTE COLLECTIBLES

RELIGIOUS THEMES

The relationship between Roman Catholicism and Italy's artists and sculptors has undergone numerous shifts through the centuries. Although Capodimonte porcelain has never been greatly influenced by religious themes, figurines are being produced that remind Christians of the meaning of their faith.

Perhaps the most popular religious figures are of the Madonna and Christ Child. Several sculptors have also done Pietàs, poignant images of the Virgin Mary mourning over the body of her crucified Son.

Biblical stories are also used as themes. Figurines and groups of figurines show the struggle between David and Goliath or the temptation of Adam and Eve in the Garden of Eden.

A number of current pastoral figurines include a small roadside shrine similar to the ones where the faithful prayed while on pilgrimage. Now, maidens are shown bringing bouquets of flowers along with their prayers.

THE "MADONNA" CLEARLY REVEALS THE INFLUENCE OF THE GREAT MASTERS OF THE ITALIAN RENAISSANCE. NOTICE HER PLACID EXPRESSION AND THE DETAILING OF HER MANTLE AND CROWN.

THIS "PIETÀ" BY L. BENACCHIO FOR TRIADE IS AN UNUSUAL
AND COMPELLING WORK OF ART.
RATHER THAN BENDING HER HEAD IN SORROW, BENACCHIO'S MARY LOOKS OUTWARD
AND HER ARMS ARE EXTENDED AS IF TO GATHER
ALL THE BROKEN AND DYING HUMANITY TO HER HEART.
NOTEWORTHY, TOO, IS THE INCLUSION OF YOUNG INNOCENT FIGURES
INTO THIS TRAGIC SCENE.
BENACCHIO DIED IN 1989, AND TRIADE WAS CLOSED.

CAPODIMONTE COLLECTIBLES

TRADITIONAL IN COMPOSITION, TIZIANO GALLI'S "PIETÀ"
IS REMINISCENT OF
MICHELANGELO'S FAMOUS WORK BY THE SAME NAME.
THE BODY OF CHRIST SEEMS FRAIL
AND ALMOST CHILDLIKE
AS MARY LOOKS DOWN ON HIS BROKEN BODY.

A MAJOR WORK IN THE CAPODIMONTE GENRE,
"THE NATIVITY," BY LUCIANO CAZZOLA FOR PORCELLANE PRINCIPE,
OFFERS A PANORAMIC VIEW OF THE CHRIST CHILD'S BIRTH.
INSTEAD OF FOCUSING ON THE HUMBLE STABLE,
CAZZOLA HAS PLACED THE HOLY FAMILY IN THE MIDST
OF VAULTING ARCHES, MARBLE COLUMNS, AND GREENERY.
MORE THAN 100 SEPARATE MOLDS
WERE NEEDED TO PRODUCE THIS WORK OF ART.
THIS IS A LIMITED EDITION OF 500 FIGURINES.

CAPODIMONTE COLLECTIBLES

THE ATTENTION OF JOSEPH AND MARY IS FOCUSED ON THE INFANT
SITTING IN MARY'S LAP.
AT HER FEET, WE SEE A YOUNG SHEPHERD WITH HIS RAM.
ON ONE SIDE OF THE HOLY FAMILY, A PEASANT WOMAN FEEDS HER CHICKENS,
PROBABLY UNAWARE OF THE MOMENTOUS NATURE OF THE OCCASION.
ON THE OTHER SIDE, WE FIND A GENTLEWOMAN AND A YOUNG BOY ON HORSEBACK
TRAVELING ACROSS THE ROCKY TERRAIN TO VISIT THE CHRIST CHILD.
NOTICE THE WAY IN WHICH SMALL ANIMALS,
FLOWERS, AND SHRUBBERY COMPLETE THIS WORK.

CAPODIMONTE COLLECTIBLES

TIZIANO GALLI HAS DONE
JUSTICE TO THE STORY OF
ADAM AND EVE IN THE
GARDEN OF EDEN.
IRONICALLY, ADAM
LIES PROSTRATE ON THE
GROUND AS EVE
LISTENS TO THE SERPENT'S
SWEET WORDS.
SHE PLUCKS AN APPLE FROM
THE BRANCH ABOVE HER HEAD.
THE BEAUTIFUL EVE
JOINS HANDS WITH ADAM
AS SHE GIVES HIM
THE FORBIDDEN FRUIT.
MISSING FROM THE SCENE IS
ANY LOATHING AT THE
SIGHT OF THE SERPENT.

TIZIANO GALLI'S TRADEMARK.

"DAVID AND GOLIATH,"
SCULPTED BY TIZIANO GALLI,
LEAVES NO QUESTION
OF THE MALEVOLENT RAGE OF
THE GIANT GOLIATH.
SKILLED AS A WARRIOR,
HIS SHIELD AND
TWO-EDGED SABER HAVE
DEFENDED HIM AGAINST ALL
HIS OPPONENTS.
UNPROTECTED BY SHIELD OR
ARMOR, YOUNG DAVID PREPARES
TO VANQUISH HIS ENEMY WITH
HIS ONLY WEAPON.
NOTICE GALLI'S SKILL AT
PORTRAYING THE HUMAN FIGURE
AND THE DETAILING ON
GOLIATH'S WEAPONS.

THIS "CHRIST HEAD,"
SCULPTED BY LUCIANO CAZZOLA
FOR PORCELLANE PRINCIPE,
IS A WELL-EXECUTED
TRADITIONAL PIECE.
THE TRAUMA OF THE CRUCIFIXION
BEHIND HIM,
CHRIST'S FACE HAS BEEN
CLEANSED OF THE SWEAT AND
BLOOD THAT MARRED IT
DURING HIS JOURNEY TO CALVARY.
ONLY HIS CROWN OF THORNS
REMAINS AS A REMINDER
OF HIS STRUGGLE.

THIS "MADONNA," BY
TIZIANO GALLI, IS THE
SENTIMENTAL PORTRAYAL OF
THE MADONNA AND CHILD THAT
HAS BEEN POPULAR
THROUGH THE CENTURIES.
THE TENDER FEELING BETWEEN
THESE FIGURES HAS BEEN
IDEALIZED AND EMBELLISHED.
A HALO DECORATED BY
GOLDEN STARS SEEMS AN
APPROPRIATE DECORATIVE TOUCH.

THIS BAS-RELIEF "PIETÀ," BY
LUCIANO CAZZOLA
FOR PORCELLANE PRINCIPE,
SHOWS MARY AND THE
CRUCIFIED CHRIST
AGAINST A LANDSCAPE OF ROCKS
AND DESERT PALMS.
HER ARMS ARE OUTSTRETCHED,
AND THE PAIN AND
ANGUISH IN HER FACE
ARE CONCEALED FROM THOSE
WHO INTRUDE ON THIS
TRAGIC SCENE.

BARBETTA'S "MADONNA,"
PRODUCED BY FLAVIA, REVEALS
THE ARTIST'S SKILL IN
HANDLING THE HUMAN FIGURE
IN THE ANCIENT TRADITION.
THERE IS AN UNUSUAL SWEETNESS
ABOUT THE MADONNA'S FACE,
AND THE CHILD SEEMS
SO REAL THAT WE EXPECT HIM
TO TRY TO ELUDE HIS
MOTHER'S GRASP.
THE SIMPLICITY OF MARY'S GOWN
IS ENHANCED BY BARBETTA'S
MASTERY OF THE LIGHT
AND SHADOWS FORMED IN THE
FOLDS OF HER CLOTHING.

THE TRADEMARK FOR BARBETTA
OF FLAVIA.

SCULPTED BY LUCIANO CAZZOLA FOR PORCELLANE PRINCIPE, "MINUET"
IS A SUPERB PORTRAYAL OF THE GLAMOROUS ENTERTAINMENTS PROVIDED AT COURT.
BOTH FIGURES WEAR ELABORATE POWDERED WIGS.
THE FITTED BODICE OF THE PRETTY YOUNG WOMAN'S GOWN IS
DECORATED WITH A NOSEGAY, AND HER PETTICOAT AND
HER HOOPED SKIRT ARE ELABORATE.
THE GENTLEMAN DISPLAYS RUFFLES ON THE FRONT OF HIS SHIRT,
AND HIS SCARLET COAT AND BLACK BREECHES ARE DECORATED WITH GOLD BUTTONS.

CAPODIMONTE COLLECTIBLES

COURTLY SPLENDOR

For King Charles and his descendants, the royal court was the hub of the universe. While he was amused by the vitality of the actors, clowns, and fishermen whom the early artists used as models, there is no question that the wealth and power of Europe's royal families profoundly influenced the art he wished to produce.

Charles and his son Ferdinand ensured that life in their courts was portrayed with the same elegance and flair seen at the French court at Versailles. The women were always young and beautiful, and their layers of petticoats were topped with elegant gowns of brocade and silk decorated with handmade laces, ribbons, and flowers. The emotions of these courtly figures are rarely revealed. None of their trials or triumphs can be discerned from their facial expressions or body language.

These elegant lords and ladies still appear in Capodimonte figurines being produced today. Gallant gentlemen, wearing the traditional powdered wig tied back with a ribbon, bow to their elaborately gowned dancing partners. Great care is taken to recreate accurately the brocades and ruffles of their costumes, fine jewelry, and fans.

Decades after the royal porcelain factory at Capodimonte was closed, many of the original Capodimonte molds were purchased by the Ginori factory. They were incorporated into the Ginori line until the late 19th century, when they were retired. In recent years, the Richard-Ginori company has resumed production of a select number of porcelains using the original Capodimonte molds. Although these figurines have not yet been marketed in the United States, many determined collectors have purchased these figurines in Italy and brought them back to their collections in America.

THIS UNPAINTED PORCELAIN FIGURINE FROM RICHARD-GINORI IS BASED
ON ALEXANDER DUMAS' POPULAR HEROES THE MUSKETEERS (I MOSCHETTIERI).
THEY ARE REPRODUCTIONS OF FIGURES FROM THE 1838-1878 PERIOD
OF THE MANIFATTURA DI DOCCIA.
LIKE THE EARLY CAPODIMONTE FIGURINES, THESE FIGURINES REFLECT
AN INTEREST IN THE COURTLY LIFE.
THEY REVEAL THE SCULPTOR'S ABILITY TO RECREATE REAL-LIFE FIGURES
WHO SWAGGER, BOW, AND SPEAK WITH EASE.
EVEN THE FOLD OF THEIR UNIFORMS AND THE PLUMES ON THEIR HATS
SEEM TO COME TO LIFE IN THE SCULPTOR'S HANDS.

TAKEN FROM "I MARESCIALLI," A SERIES OF SIX FIGURINES INSPIRED
BY THE NAPOLEONIC ERA, THIS FIGURINE, "LASALLE,"
REVEALS THE ARTIST'S SKILL AND ABILITY TO DRAW FROM REALITY.
IT IS SHOWN HERE HAND-PAINTED AND UNPAINTED.
AFTER THE CAPODIMONTE MOLDS WERE ACQUIRED BY THE
PORCELLANE ARTISTICA DI DOCCIA,
THESE FIGURINES WERE ORIGINALLY PRODUCED DURING THE PERIOD 1848–1878.
THE ORIGINALS ARE DISPLAYED AT THE MUSEO DELLE PORCELLANE
DI DOCCIA IN FLORENCE, AND THESE REPRODUCTIONS
HAVE BEEN PRODUCED ON A LIMITED BASIS BY THE RICHARD-GINORI CORPORATION.

THE TRADEMARK FOR IPA.

"MUSKETEER DUEL," BY GIORGIO PELLATI FOR IPA, SHOWS
TWO GENTLEMEN ENGAGED IN A DUEL OF HONOR.
IN SPITE OF ONE PARTICIPANT'S MISFORTUNE IN FALLING
DOWN A FLIGHT OF STAIRS, THE HIGHLY STYLIZED MOVEMENTS OF
THE OTHER COMBATANT MUST NEVER BE INTERRUPTED.
THE GENTLEMAN IN THE SCARLET DOUBLET AND BLACK HAT WITH FEATHERS
HAS BEEN CAREFULLY CRAFTED
TO RECREATE THE COSTUMES OF THE PERIOD.

CAPODIMONTE COLLECTIBLES

"MY GALLANT LOVE," BY GIORGIO PELLATI FOR IPA, FEATURES
A YOUNG PEASANT MAIDEN CARRYING A BASKET OF FLOWERS
AND A GENTLEMAN ASTRIDE A WHITE HORSE.
OBVIOUSLY FLATTERED BY THE GENTLEMAN'S ATTENTIONS,
SHE DREAMS OF ROMANCE.
A FINELY DETAILED FIGURINE, THIS WORK
IS AN EXCELLENT EXAMPLE OF CAPODIMONTE CRAFTMANSHIP.

"LADY WITH DOVES," SCULPTED BY CESARE MOLLICA
AND ISSUED BY PORCELLANE PRINCIPE,
IS AN ELEGANT EXAMPLE OF THE FASHIONS AND MANNERS OF COURT LIFE.
THE WOMAN'S ELABORATE HAIRSTYLE AND FULL SKIRT AND PETTICOAT
REVEAL HER WEALTH AND RANK.
TO FURTHER EMBELLISH THIS WORK,
THE ARTIST HAS ADDED A GOLD PATTERN TO THE BASE.

CAPODIMONTE COLLECTIBLES

"LADY AND GALLANT," BY CESARE MOLLICA,
IS A HIGHLY STYLIZED FIGURINE THAT SHOWS THE PRECISION OF
A TRUE MASTER OF THIS GENRE.
NOTICE THE FINE DETAILING ON
THE GENTLEMAN'S JACKET
AND THE BUCKLES ON HIS SLIPPERS.

CAPODIMONTE COLLECTIBLES

"LADY WITH MIRROR," BY GIORGIO PELLATI
FOR IPA, IS DRESSED
IN A TURN-OF-THE-CENTURY COSTUME.
FROM THE ORNAMENTS ON HER HAT TO THE TINY
RUFFLES ON THE HEM OF HER SKIRT,
EVERY DETAIL HAS BEEN CAREFULLY EXECUTED.

GINO PEZZATO'S "CAVALIER" IS A TRIM YOUNG MAN DRESSED
IN WHITE BREECHES AND A BLUE COAT
FROM THE NAPOLEONIC PERIOD.
HIS HEAD APPEARS TO BE SMALL FOR HIS BODY,
AS WAS TRUE OF THE EARLIEST CAPODIMONTE FIGURINES.
NOTICE THE ALMOST TRADITIONAL USE OF SMALL FLOWERS AT HIS FEET.

"LADY VICTORIA," BY GIORGIO PELLATI FOR IPA,
IS A LOVELY, DETAILED FIGURINE.
THE LEG-OF-MUTTON SLEEVES COMPLEMENT HER
WASP WAIST AND GENTLY DRAPED FLOOR-LENGTH COAT.
SHE CARRIES A MATCHING PARASOL AND
PEERS THROUGH HER LORGNETTE.

"LADY IMPERIAL STYLE," ALSO BY GINO PEZZATO,
IS A COMPANION PIECE TO "CAVALIER."
THIS BEAUTY IS WEARING A SIMPLE GOWN AND
IS AN EXTREMELY GRACEFUL FIGURE,
AND HER HEAD APPEARS TO BE SMALL AND SIMILAR IN APPEARANCE
TO THE EARLY CAPODIMONTE FIGURES MODELED BY GRICCI.

"BOY ON DONKEY," BY LUCIANO CAZZOLA FOR PORCELLANE PRINCIPE,
IS AN EXAMPLE OF A LIGHTHEARTED PASTORAL SCENE.
A YOUNG BOY IS RIDING BACKWARD ON HIS DONKEY.
HIS HAT MAY BE TATTERED
AND HIS SHIRT RAGGED, BUT HE HOLDS UP
HIS BUNCH OF GRAPES WITH ENJOYMENT AND ANTICIPATION.

PASTORAL SCENES

Italy's political turmoil and the closing of the royal Capodimonte factory forced the modelers and workers to ply their trade in the hundreds of small porcelain factories throughout the countryside. Cut off from royal patronage, the artisans drew their inspiration from the rural world around them. The powdered wigs and brocades of the royal court gave way to the tattered shirts and skirts of sturdy country folk.

Porcelain artists created a pastoral paradise with no rainy days or lost lambs. Young shepherds tended their flocks in peace, and maidens gathered flowers in a land that was always sunny. Despite this idealized setting, most of the pastoral figurines are more lifelike than those of courtly splendor. Their facial expressions and their movements reveal their character and activities.

Porcelain hunters and fishermen test their skills outdoors. Card-players gathered around a table provide jovial insights into everyday camaraderie. The artist, the pharmacist, the dentist, and the doctor all find their professions immortalized along with the veterinarian, the cobbler, and the baker.

A line of pastoral figurines that is extremely popular with American collectors has been produced by Giuseppe Armani for Florence Sculture d'Arte. Made of cold-cast porcelain (see page 191), the figurines of peasant children have a naiveté and playfulness that is endearing. The adult figurines are particularly sophisticated and romantic. DEAR Sculture Artistiche also produces cold-cast porcelain. A finely detailed figurine by their sculptor Auro Belcari shows a girl holding a basket of rosebuds. The facial expression and the ruffled gown show how modern technology can produce extremely fine detailing.

"THE ESSENCE OF SPRING," BY BARBETTA FOR FLAVIA,
PROVIDES US WITH A GLIMPSE INTO THE FRESH NEW WORLD INHABITED BY PASTORAL LOVERS.
ROSE BLOSSOMS SLIP FROM THE YOUNG WOMAN'S LAP
AS SHE LISTENS TO THE YOUNG MAN SEATED AT HER SIDE.
NONE OF LIFE'S DISAPPOINTMENTS
CAN REACH THEM IN THE SECRET WORLD THAT THEY ALONE INHABIT.

CAPPÉ'S WORKS FOR ROYAL
CROWN PORCELAIN ARE MARKED
WITH HIS SIGNATURE.

TONGUE IN CHEEK, GIUSEPPE CAPPÉ
REVEALS THE PREOCCUPATION OF TWO GENTLEMEN SHARING
THEIR "OPEN-AIR BREAKFAST."
ALL THOUGHTS OF FOOD ARE FORGOTTEN
AS THEY GAZE AT THE AMPLE SWELL OF THE BODICE OF THE WAITRESS.

CAPODIMONTE COLLECTIBLES

LUCIANO CAZZOLA'S
"THE PAINTER," PRODUCED BY
PORCELLANE PRINCIPE,
SHOWS A PROFESSIONAL ARTIST
WHO HAS LEFT HIS STUDIO
TO WORK OUTDOORS.
THE GESTURE OF HIS ARM
INDICATES THAT THIS MAY BE
THE DAY HE CREATES
HIS MASTERPIECE.
BESIDE HIM IS HIS PAINT BOX
WITH ITS ROLLED-UP
TUBES OF PAINT
AND HIS STAINED PAINT RAGS.

"THE SHOE MENDER," BY GINO PEZZATO,
CAPTURES A MIDDLE-AGED SHOE REPAIRMAN
BUSY AT HIS WORKBENCH.
A MASTER OF THE HUMAN FORM, PEZZATO
ENABLES US TO SEE THE POWERFUL MOVEMENTS
NEEDED TO REPAIR LEATHER.
THE SHOE REPAIRMAN HAS THE WITHDRAWN
FACIAL EXPRESSION OF A MAN WHO
IS ABSORBED IN HIS WORK.

"OUT FOR A WALK," BY GINO PEZZATO, INTRODUCES US TO A SMALL GROUP OF CHILDREN ENTERTAINING THEMSELVES WITH A WALK.

A YOUNG BOY IN A SAILOR'S SUIT TAKES TIME TO RIDE THE FENCE, WHILE THE GIRLS CONFINE THEIR INTEREST TO THE FLOWERS AND THE YOUNG LAMBS THAT PRECEDE THEM DOWN THE PATH.

"LITTLE GIRL AND COCK," BY LUCIANO CAZZOLA FOR PORCELLANE PRINCIPE, SHOWS THE LITTLE GIRL STEPPING GRACEFULLY INTO THE BARNYARD WITH HER BASKET OF GRAIN. SHE PROBABLY FEEDS THE CHICKENS REGULARLY, BECAUSE THE COCK IS RUNNING TO GREET HER.

CAPODIMONTE COLLECTIBLES

THE TRADEMARK FOR
PORCELLANE PRINCIPE.

"A DAY ON THE FARM" ("UN GIORNO ALLA FATTORIA"),
SCULPTED BY LUCIANO CAZZOLA FOR PORCELLANE PRINCIPE,
CAPTURES THE PEACE AND SUNSHINE OF COUNTRY LIFE.
THE MOTHER AND DAUGHTER TAKE TIME OUT FROM THEIR
WORK TO ENJOY THE DAY.

"YOUNG RASCALS WITH DONKEY," BY LUCIANO CAZZOLA
FOR PORCELLANE PRINCIPE, IS A CHARMING AND FINELY DETAILED
LOOK AT YOUNG BOYS AT PLAY.
THEY MEAN NO HARM TO THE DONKEY THEY HAVE CAPTURED
TO RIDE AROUND THE FARMYARD.

"THE GRAPE HARVEST" ("LA VENDEMMIA") IS A MASTERPIECE
SCULPTED BY LUCIANO CAZZOLA IN 1981 FOR PORCELLANE PRINCIPE.
THIS LARGE, MULTI-FIGURED PORCELAIN IS A LIMITED EDITION OF 500 PIECES.
IT DEPICTS THE CELEBRATIONS THAT ACCOMPANY THE GRAPE HARVEST
AND THE SUBSEQUENT WINE-MAKING.
RIPE APPLES ON A TREE AND A TRELLIS LOADED WITH GRAPES SERVE AS A BACKDROP.
THE CENTRAL FIGURE IS A YOUNG WOMAN
CARRYING TWO BASKETS OF GRAPES.
ANOTHER GIRL PICKS A CLUSTER OF GRAPES FROM THE TRELLIS.

TWO YOUNG MEN HELP FILL THE WINE PRESS WITH GRAPES, WHILE AN OLDER GENTLEMAN
CHECKS THE SPIGOT AND ASSEMBLES THE JUGS TO BE FILLED WITH JUICE.
THE GRANDMOTHER SITS WITH A TRAY HOLDING BREAD, WINE, AND CHEESE
TO FEED THE HUNGRY WORKERS.
UNCONCERNED WITH ALL THE PREPARATIONS, A YOUNG BOY PURSUES A RABBIT.
NOTICE THE DETAILING ON THE WINE PRESS,
THE JUGS, AND THE PIECES OF CROCKERY SCATTERED AROUND THE BARNYARD.
CONTRAST THE LOOK OF PLEASURE ON THE FACES OF THE TWO WOMEN
WITH THE LOOK ON THE GRANDMOTHER'S FACE
AS SHE WATCHES THE TRAY BEGIN TO SLIDE WHEN THE BOY GRABS HER APRON.

LUCIANO CAZZOLA'S "JEWELER," PRODUCED BY PORCELLANE PRINCIPE,
SHOWS THE TRADE OF AN EXPERT IN PEARLS AND GEMS.
NOTICE THE CASUAL WAY THAT HE SITS,
TOTALLY UNIMPRESSED BY THE BAUBLES
THAT ROUTINELY PASS THROUGH HIS HANDS.

IN "FLOWER ARRANGEMENT," FROM DEAR'S CLASSIC SERIES,
AURO BELCARI HAS SCULPTED A DECEPTIVELY SIMPLE PIECE THAT IS
SURPRISINGLY DETAILED WHILE RETAINING A DREAMY, ROMANTIC AMBIENCE.
THE COLD-CAST PORCELAIN USED IN THIS FIGURINE AND
THE METICULOUS HAND-PAINTING CREATE THE DETAIL IN HER FACIAL EXPRESSION,
THE FOLDS OF HER SKIRT, AND THE BASKET OF ROSES.

CAPODIMONTE COLLECTIBLES

"SHOEMAKER WITH GIRL," SCULPTED BY LUCIANO CAZZOLA AND PRODUCED BY PORCELLANE PRINCIPE, SHOWS AN UNLIKELY COMBINATION. MOST OF THE SHOEMAKER'S CUSTOMERS ARE WORKMEN WHOSE BOOTS NEED MENDING OR HOUSEWIVES TRYING TO MAKE SHOES LAST JUST ONE MORE SEASON. HE APPEARS PUZZLED AS HE LISTENS TO THIS BEAUTIFUL YOUNG WOMAN. AMONG THE CLUTTER OF HIS WORKBENCH, CAN HE FIND WHAT IS NEEDED TO SOLVE HER PROBLEM?

"COUNTRY GIRL," MADE OF COLD-CAST PORCELAIN BY GIUSEPPE ARMANI FOR FLORENCE SCULTURE D'ARTE, SHOWS A YOUNG WOMAN AND A SMALL GIRL PLACING A FLORAL OFFERING AT A ROADSIDE SHRINE. THESE TRADITIONAL SHRINES ATTRACT TRAVELERS PRAYING FOR SAFE JOURNEYS. NOTICE THE STYLIZED SHRUBBERY THAT ENHANCES THE STRONG VERTICAL MOVEMENT OF THIS FIGURINE.

IN "THE GAME OF CARDS,"
BY GIUSEPPE CAPPÉ, WE SEE
THREE OLD FRIENDS WHO,
FOR DECADES, HAVE BEEN
GATHERING TO PLAY A FRIENDLY
GAME OF CARDS.
THEIR FACES ARE MASKED BY
EXPRESSIONS THAT THEY
HOPE WILL MISLEAD THEIR
FELLOW PLAYERS.
WHILE THE GAME CONTINUES
ENDLESSLY, A KITTEN ARRIVES
TO REMIND ITS OWNER THAT
IT'S MEALTIME.

GIUSEPPE ARMANI'S LEAN AND LANGUID
FIGURES HAVE CREATED SOME OF
THE MOST SOPHISTICATED AND ROMANTIC
PASTORAL IMAGES.
IN "SERENADE," PRODUCED IN COLD-CAST
PORCELAIN BY FLORENCE SCULTURE
D'ARTE, WE SEE A YOUNG MAN
SERENADING HIS LOVE ON A MANDOLIN.
OVERHEAD, A GENTLE BREEZE DRIFTS
THROUGH THE LEAVES OF A PALM TREE ON
THIS TROPICAL PARADISE.

CAPODIMONTE COLLECTIBLES

THE KING'S PORCELAIN
TRADEMARK.

IN "WEARY HUNTER," GIUSEPPE CAPPÉ CAPTURES THE BONE-TIRED STEPS
OF A HUNTER WHO HAS BEEN LESS THAN SUCCESSFUL
IN BRINGING HOME HIS EVENING MEAL.
HE MIGHT BE THINKING OF THE TALE HE MUST SPIN TO KEEP HIS FELLOW HUNTERS
FROM KNOWING THAT HIS TRIP ENDED IN FAILURE.

GIUSEPPE CAPPÉ HAS NOT FALSELY ROMANTICIZED "GYPSY WOMAN";
THERE IS NOTHING PRETTY ABOUT THE POVERTY AND GRIME THAT SEEMS TO CLING
TO HER THREE CHILDREN SURROUNDING HER.
YET CAPPÉ HAS CAPTURED SOMETHING ALMOST HEROIC IN HER STANCE.
WE FEEL THAT SHE WILL NEVER FALL PREY TO SELF-PITY OR ANGER.

CAPODIMONTE COLLECTIBLES

"OUR GRANDMOTHER'S TREAT" IS A RICHLY DETAILED
TABLEAU BY ANTONIO BORSATO.
THIS SCULPTURE CAPTURES THE UNIQUE BOND BETWEEN
GRANDMOTHERS AND THEIR YOUNG GRANDCHILDREN.
FROM THE BRICKS ON THE WALLS TO ALL THE POTS AND PANS,
BORSATO HAS CAREFULLY CRAFTED THIS HUMBLE PEASANT HOME.

"BREAD MAKER," BY LUCIANO CAZZOLA FOR PORCELLANE PRINCIPE,
PROVIDES US WITH A CLOSE-UP LOOK AT THE BAKER'S CRAFT.
FROM THE ARCH OF THE BRICKS ON THE FRONT OF THE OVEN
TO THE WOVEN BASKET FILLED WITH LOAVES OF BREAD,
ALL THE DETAILS CONTRIBUTE TO THIS PLEASING VIEW
OF THE BREAD MAKER'S TRADE.

IN GIUSEPPE ARMANI'S
FIGURINE "LADY WITH GRAPE
WAGON," PRODUCED IN
COLD-CAST PORCELAIN BY
FLORENCE SCULTURE D'ARTE,
WE SEE THE INNOCENCE AND
BEAUTY OF A YOUNG GIRL. BOTH
THE CART AND HER DRESS WITH
APRON ARE CAREFULLY
DETAILED, AND HER FACIAL
EXPRESSION IS VERY APPEALING.

LUCIANO CAZZOLA'S "THE HUNTER" ("IL CACCIATORE"), PRODUCED BY
PORCELLANE PRINCIPE, IS A TRULY REMARKABLE PORCELAIN FIGURINE.
IT COMBINES ENERGETIC IMAGES OF A HUMAN FIGURE, A DOG, DUCKS,
AND THE SURROUNDING GROUND AND SHRUBBERY.
EACH OF THESE ELEMENTS CONTAINS ENOUGH VITALITY AND DETAILING
TO STAND ALONE.
TOGETHER, THEY PROVIDE AN INTERESTING STUDY IN THE ART OF HUNTING.

GIUSEPPE ARMANI, A PIONEER IN COLD-CAST PORCELAIN, HAS SCULPTED THIS CHARMING BUCOLIC FIGURINE FROM THE ARMANI COLLECTION FOR FLORENCE SCULTURE D'ARTE. "COUPLE BY WALL" SHOWS A PLEASANT MEETING BETWEEN TWO LOVERS. NOTICE THE HANDPAINTED FACIAL EXPRESSIONS, THE ELEGANT FOLDS IN THE GIRL'S SKIRT, AND THE BOY'S RUMPLED HAT.

"BIG FISHERMAN" ("IL PESCATORE"), BY CAZZOLA,
IS A COMPANION PIECE TO "THE HUNTER."
THE ARTIST HAS COMBINED A HUMAN FIGURE WITH DEPICTIONS
OF AN ANIMAL, A FISH, AND THE ACCOMPANYING SHRUBBERY.
NOTICE THE REALISM IN THE FISHERMAN'S STANCE AND THE WAY
THAT HIS COMPANION RESPONDS
TO THE FISH THAT DIDN'T GET AWAY.

"LADY WITH BICYCLE" SHOWS A TALL, SLENDER YOUNG WOMAN WEARING
A 1930S-STYLE FROCK AND WIDE-BRIMMED HAT.
A SPRING BREEZE IS ABOUT TO CARRY OFF HER HAT AS SHE PAUSES FOR A MOMENT
BEFORE CONTINUING HER BICYCLE JOURNEY.
THIS FIGURINE, MADE OF COLD-CAST PORCELAIN BY GIUSEPPE ARMANI
FOR FLORENCE SCULTURE D'ARTE,
IS THE "SPRING" OFFERING IN THE "FOUR SEASONS" SERIES.

MODERN REALISM

Some experts believe that the only authentic Capodimonte porcelains are the ones that depict stylized court life and bucolic scenes. But the early works of King Charles's artisans refute this premise. Charles clearly challenged his artists to explore new subjects and new techniques.

DELICATE HAND-PAINTING
CREATES THE BEAUTY OF
THE YOUNG WOMAN'S FACE.

There were subtle hints of irony and black humor in the early Capodimonte pieces. In exploring the same tragic, comic, and absurd aspects of life, Giuseppe Cappé breaks new ground as one of the few artists willing to create figures that are less than ideal. In creating his mature gentlemen with bald spots and paunches, his touch is so deft and his humor so infectious that his characters seem to come to life. In a world where old age is largely overlooked, Cappé can look beyond the wrinkles to see the virtues of love, companionship, and caring.

During the all-too-brief period in which porcelains were produced at Capodimonte, there were decided shifts in technique and subjects. Given this progress, it is not surprising that the Capodimonte genre has grown and changed as new artists have continued to search for new formulas and subjects.

One of the most interesting new subjects has been the introduction of striking young women in modern dress. Highly stylized and sophisticated, these modern figurines are prized by some collectors who believe that they represent the type of figurines that the king's artisans would be producing today. The idealized figures of Giuseppe Armani, in a new material called cold-cast porcelain (see page 191), have graceful, flowing lines and are decorated in clear, soft colors that give them a fresh, youthful appearance. Like their predecessors at the royal court, all the women are tall, slender, beautiful, and young.

"TELEPHONE" IS FROM THE
GIUSEPPE ARMANI "COUPLES"
SERIES PRODUCED IN
COLD-CAST PORCELAIN BY
FLORENCE SCULTURE D'ARTE.
AT THIS TIME,
ALL THE FIGURINES
IN THIS SERIES,
WHICH ARE POPULAR AS
ANNIVERSARY AND
COMMEMORATIVE GIFTS,
ARE OPEN ISSUES.
ARMANI HAS SCULPTED A
HANDSOME YOUNG COUPLE IN
EVENING CLOTHES.
SEATED ON AN ORNATE STOOL,
THE LADY IS CARRYING ON
AN ANIMATED TELEPHONE
CONVERSATION, WHILE
HER COMPANION
IMPATIENTLY AWAITS.

IN THIS FIGURINE,
"MOTHER AND CHILD," FROM
THE "MY FAIR LADY" SERIES
FROM FLORENCE SCULTURE
D'ARTE, ARTIST
GIUSEPPE ARMANI IS ABLE
TO PORTRAY A FACE OF
LOVE AND BEAUTY.
THE USE OF CURVES AND
LINES IN THIS DESIGN IS
VERY SKILLFUL, BUT
IT IS THE LOOK OF LOVE
ON THE FACE OF
THE YOUNG MOTHER
THAT MAKES THE PIECE
SO APPEALING.
THIS FIGURINE IS LIMITED
TO AN EDITION OF 5,000.

CAPODIMONTE COLLECTIBLES

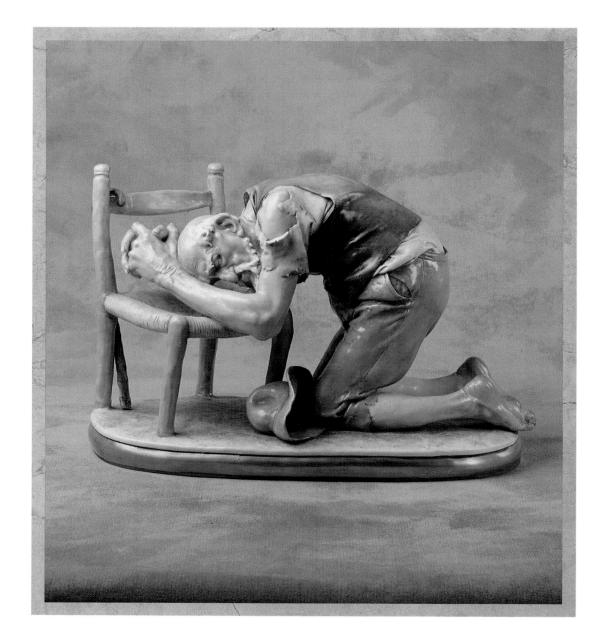

IN THE SELECTION OF HIS SUBJECTS, GIUSEPPE CAPPÉ SOMETIMES GOES BEYOND
THE BOUNDARIES OF WHAT IS NORMALLY CONSIDERED CAPODIMONTE ART.
HE SHOWS US BEAUTY AND PATHOS IN THIS
HUMBLE OLD MAN AT PRAYER.
SCULPTED BY CAPPÉ IN 1965 AND PRODUCED
BY ROYAL CROWN PORCELAIN, "PRAYER" SHOWS
A LABORER WITH BIG HANDS LINED WITH YEARS OF TOIL.
HIS HAT IS BATTERED, HIS SHIRT IS TORN, AND HE IS SHOELESS.
IN HIS SIMPLICITY AND FAITH HE BOWS HIS HEAD IN PRAYER.

"PEACOCK LADY" IS SCULPTED IN
COLD-CAST PORCELAIN BY GIUSEPPE
ARMANI FOR THE "MY FAIR LADY"
SERIES OF FLORENCE SCULTURE D'ARTE.
THIS TALL, LANGUID BEAUTY CARRYING
A PEACOCK ON HER SHOULDER EVOKES
ALL KINDS OF FANTASIES.
THIS FIGURINE IS LIMITED TO
AN EDITION SIZE OF 5,000.

"LADY WITH FUR," BY LUCIANO
CAZZOLA, IS ONE OF THE
FIGURINES PRODUCED
BY PORCELLANE PRINCIPE
ESPECIALLY FOR AFRICAN-AMERICAN
COLLECTORS OF CAPODIMONTE.
THIS BEAUTIFUL WOMAN, CARRYING
A FUR DRAPED OVER ONE ARM,
IS CHIC AND ELEGANT.

IN "THE BATTLE" ("LA BATTAGLIA"), A 1970 SCULPTURE BY
GIUSEPPE CAPPÉ FOR ROYAL CROWN PORCELAIN,
THE ULTIMATE STRUGGLE FOR VICTORY
IS TAKING PLACE BEFORE OUR EYES.
STALLIONS AND SOLDIERS ARE ENTWINED IN A FRENZIED COMBAT, WITH
THE HOOVES OF THE WHITE HORSE AS DANGEROUS A WEAPON
AS THE SOLDIER'S SWORD.

CAPODIMONTE COLLECTIBLES

WILDLIFE

Birds and animals rarely appeared in the mythological, theatrical, and grotesque images produced by the early Capodimonte artists. But as the simple pleasures of the court and bourgeoise began to emerge as a theme during the reign of King Ferdinand IV, birds and animals were gradually included. The family's pet—a terrier or perhaps a wolfhound—was added to the grouping of a family strolling through the park. A pair of lovebirds added a romantic touch to the meeting of young lovers, and a fluffy kitten became the attentive companion of a young beauty.

The official closing of the royal Capodimonte factory in the early 1800s was the catalyst that radically changed the Capodimonte art. Most master artists and modelers were suddenly forced to ply their trade in smaller porcelain factories throughout the countryside. Cut off from the wealth and patronage of the court, the focus of their art shifted from powdered wigs and hooped skirts to the earthy pastoral scenes that surrounded them. The jovial gatherings around a card table, or the festivities surrounding the harvesting of the grapes, attracted the artists' attention.

But it was not only the fascinating personalities that captured the artists' imagination. Suddenly, the menagerie of barnyard fowl and animals came into their own. A pair of chickens could be seen scratching in the dust of the courtyard. Soon, a parade of pigs, ducks, geese, and dogs—all the creatures common to the rural Italian landscape—were a part of the bucolic scenes of Capodimonte.

No attempt was made to idealize these humble birds and animals. A dog might be scratching his fleas, sniffing a tree, or gazing in admiration at his master. Pigs rooting in the mud and rabbits nibbling the lettuce completed the pastoral milieu without overpowering it.

"CHICKEN HOUSE," BY LUCIANO CAZZOLA FOR PORCELLANE PRINCIPE, IS
AN INTRIGUING EXAMPLE OF THE CURRENT CAPODIMONTE ART.
WHILE THE OLD LADY GATHERING EGGS IS CHARMING,
THIS FIGURINE HAS BEEN MADE MUCH
MORE IMPRESSIVE WITH THE ADDITION OF A FINELY DETAILED
HEN SITTING ON A BUNDLE OF STRAW.

CAPODIMONTE COLLECTIBLES

In "Don Quixote and Sancho Panza," by Enzo Arzenton
for the Laurenz Classic Collection, Don Quixote displays
none of the fear and bewilderment seen on the face of his servant Sancho Panza.
The knight's horse and Sancho Panza's burro
have their teeth bared in a grin.
This piece has been produced in a limited edition of 1,200.

CAPODIMONTE COLLECTIBLES

In "Countryman Costume," by
Giuseppe Cappé for
Royal Crown Porcelain,
we see an example of
the barnyard fowl being
included into the scene.
An old peasant smokes
his pipe and observes with
amusement as a pair of
chickens scratches
for seeds.

BRUNO MERLI'S FIGURINE OF
DON QUIXOTE FOR
KING'S PORCELAIN
UNDERLINES THE TRAGICOMIC
DILEMMA OF THE OLD
GENTLEMAN COMSUMED BY
THE ROMANTIC TRADITIONS
OF COURTLY LOVE
AND KNIGHTHOOD.
HIS ANCIENT STEED
STRUGGLING UNDER HIS
WEIGHT, DON QUIXOTE
SEARCHES FOR ONE MORE
HONORABLE BATTLE..
THE EVER-FAITHFUL SANCHO
PANZA STRUGGLES TO
KEEP UP WITH HIS MASTER.

THE WHIMSICAL AND REALISTIC CHARMS
OF THIS LITTLE FROG SHOW
THE TRUE ARTISTRY OF SCULPTOR
ANTONIO BORSATO.
THIS HAND-PAINTED AMPHIBIAN
LOOKS SURPRISINGLY REAL.
FROM HIS PERCH ON A LILY PAD,
THE FROG MAY BE PREPARING FOR A
LUNCH OF INSECTS, OR HE MAY BE
THE ONE WHO IS WAITING PATIENTLY
FOR THE KISS OF A PRINCESS.

CAPODIMONTE COLLECTIBLES

"RACE TO OBLIVION," BY
ANTONIO BORSATO, IS
A STRIKING AND
COMPELLING WORK.
IT SHOWS A HERD OF
FEAR-CRAZED HORSES
ASCENDING A
SPIRAL PATHWAY.
IN ADDITION TO ACHIEVING
A SENSE OF UNITY AND
BALANCE, BORSATO'S WORK
REVEALS THE TERROR OF
THE BEASTS FLEEING
FROM—AND INTO—
SOME UNKNOWN DANGER.

CAPODIMONTE COLLECTIBLES

ANIMALS

Of the animals portrayed by the Capodimonte artists, the horse seems to command the most respect and attention. A pair of chestnuts show a touch of humor as they pull a carriage containing two lovers, and the driven energy of two steeds is revealed as the hunters close in on a fox.

Other, almost mystical images of horses are provided by Antonio Borsato in the spiraling ascent of frenzied stallions climbing to some unknown fate, and the fear-crazed stallions of Cappé's "The Battle," shown on page 132, transport the viewer into the sweaty hell of the battlefield.

Dogs, too, are frequent subjects, often shown as faithful, ever-present companions. In recent years, companies such as Porcellane Principe have introduced new idealized figurines of the different breeds of setters, retrievers, and greyhounds. These figurines are more in keeping with the porcelain images produced by the traditional English porcelain factories. Small pairs of ducks, geese, pheasants, and a cow and calf have also been issued in a more contemporary style. The majestic elephant, trunk raised in triumph, is also popular with modern artists.

EACH INDIVIDUAL HORSE IN "RACE TO OBLIVION" SHOWS A FERAL INTENSITY THAT CONTRIBUTES TO THE IMPACT OF THIS HAUNTING FIGURINE.

IN 1983, LUCIANO CAZZOLA'S "FOX HUNTING" ("CACCIA ALLA VOLPE") WAS
INTRODUCED BY PORCELLANE PRINCIPE.
AN EXTREMELY LARGE, ELABORATE, WELL-THOUGHT-OUT PIECE, IT FEATURES HUNTERS
AND THEIR DOGS IN PURSUIT OF A RED FOX.
CAZZOLA HAS FULL COMMAND OF BOTH HUMAN AND ANIMAL FIGURES,
AND EACH SEEMS TO MOVE WITH GRACE AND SPEED.
A GNARLED TREE, GRASS, AND FLOWERS CONCEAL MOST
OF THE ROCKY TERRAIN.

"THE COACH," BY BRUNO MERLI FOR KING'S PORCELAIN, IS
AN AMBITIOUS AND COMPLEX FIGURINE.
TWO HORSES ARE PULLING A HANDSOME CARRIAGE IN WHICH A YOUNG COUPLE
IS ENGAGED IN AN AMOROUS TÊTE-À-TÊTE, WHILE THE DRIVER
OF THE CARRIAGE LOOKS ON IN AMUSEMENT.
THIS THEME SEEMS TO BE VERY POPULAR WITH ARTISTS.
THE DETAILING OF ALL THE FIGURES,
THE HORSES, THE CARRIAGE, AND EVEN THE YOUNG BOY PEEKING AROUND THE CORNER
MAKE THIS AN EXCEPTIONALLY NICE PIECE.

CAPODIMONTE COLLECTIBLES

ALL DOG LOVERS CAN APPRECIATE THE CARE
WITH WHICH LUCIANO CAZZOLA HAS SCULPTED THIS
ENGLISH SETTER, A HIGH-SPIRITED GAME DOG.
THIS IS ONE OF A SET OF FOUR SETTERS
FROM PORCELLANE PRINCIPE.

"DOGS AND PHEASANTS," BY CAZZOLA FOR
PORCELLANE PRINCIPE, CAPTURES THE MOMENT OF
TRUTH AS TWO BIRD DOGS FIND THEIR QUARRY.
ON POINT, THEY WILL AWAIT
THEIR MASTER'S COMMAND.

A RED RETRIEVER PRANCES BACK ACROSS THE
FIELD HOLDING A PHEASANT GENTLY IN HIS MOUTH.
SCULPTED BY CAZZOLA FOR PORCELLANE PRINCIPE,
THIS FIGURINE IS ALSO AVAILABLE AS
A WHITE AND BLACK RETRIEVER, A RED AND
WHITE RETRIEVER, AND A BLACK RETRIEVER.

THESE RABBITS ARE RESIDENTS OF A BARNYARD
WHERE THEY MINGLE WITH ROOSTERS
AND EAT FRESH CARROTS.
THIS SMALL FIGURINE IS FROM ONE OF
CAZZOLA'S FOUR-PIECE COLLECTIONS OF BIRDS
AND ANIMALS PRODUCED BY PORCELLANE PRINCIPE.

"LADY WITH A GREYHOUND," BY ANTONIO BORSATO,
IS A PLEASANT FIGURINE THAT
ACHIEVES A SENSUAL BEAUTY.
BOTH THE YOUNG WOMAN AND HER ELEGANT COMPANION,
THE GREYHOUND, SEEM TO STRETCH
AND GLIDE EFFORTLESSLY IN THIS GRACEFUL DUET.

CAPODIMONTE COLLECTIBLES

PRODUCED OF COLD-CAST
PORCELAIN WITH A WHITE
MATTE FINISH, AURO
BELCARI'S TRUMPETING
"BULL ELEPHANT" FROM
DEAR'S BISQUE
WILDLIFE SERIES IS
IMMENSELY POPULAR WITH
COLLECTORS BECAUSE
IT SEEMS TO CAPTURE THE
VITALITY, GRACE, AND
NATURAL BEAUTY OF THESE
MAGNIFICENT BEASTS.

BOTTOM, LEFT:
THE ELEPHANT'S TRUNK IS
RAISED IN A
TRIUMPHANT GESTURE.

BOTTOM, RIGHT:
LIKE MORE TRADITIONAL
CAPODIMONTE PORCELAINS,
THE COLD-CAST PORCELAIN
FIGURES BEAR THE
TRADITIONAL CAPITAL N.

CAPODIMONTE COLLECTIBLES

IN "PEGASUS," FROM DEAR'S SERIES OF FANTASY FIGURES IN COLD-CAST PORCELAIN, AURO BELCARI HAS COMBINED HIS SUPERB KNOWLEDGE OF EQUINE ANATOMY AND HIS FANCIFUL INTERPRETATION OF GREEK MYTH. BECAUSE PEGASUS'S HOOVES WERE AN IMPORTANT PART OF THE MYTH, BELCARI SELECTED THIS ANIMATED POSE, WHICH HIGHLIGHTS THE ANIMAL'S FOREFEET AND HOOVES.

BOTTOM, LEFT:
NOTICE THE BEAUTY AND SYMMETRY OF THE WING FEATHERS AND THAT THE WINGS APPEAR TO BE A NATURAL PART OF THE ANIMAL'S ANATOMY.

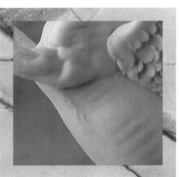

BOTTOM, RIGHT:
THE MUSCULATURE IN THE THIGHS AND RIB CAGE IS APPARENT.

CAPODIMONTE COLLECTIBLES

ONE OF THE MOST POPULAR EXAMPLES OF THE FINE DETAILING THAT CAN BE ACHIEVED WITH COLD-CAST PORCELAIN IS "HERONS," SCULPTED BY ERMANNO FARINA FOR THE DEAR WILDLIFE SERIES. THE REALISM IS APPARENT IN THE CLEAR DELINEATION OF THE FEATHERS, BEAKS, AND CLAWS.

CAPODIMONTE COLLECTIBLES

BIRDS

Among the first to master the art of sculpting birds was the late Bepi Tay (Giuseppe Tagliariol), who lived from 1915 to 1983. A child prodigy, Tay worked in the Neapolitan studio of Cacciapuoti before opening his own studio. A product of the Capodimonte influence, Tay's exquisitely sculpted birds are now coveted by discerning collectors throughout the world. Perhaps his most famous works are his "American Bald Eagle" porcelain sculptures, which were frequently presented as prized gifts of state.

In 1953, Sgr. Felice Bindi founded the Monguzzi studio on the outskirts of Monza near Milan. The factory's products were undistinguished until a decade ago, when Virgilio Bindi and his daughter Irene Bindi began gaining worldwide recognition for their fine bird and animal porcelains. Prior to joining the family business, Virgilio Bindi studied at the porcelain bird factory of Bepi Tay, and the Tay influence is apparent in his work.

The Bindi line carries a few exotic birds, although many Bindi birds are of the common varieties—wrens, robins, marsh tits, goldfinches, waxwings, and sparrows—familiar to the Italian countryside. Perched on branches or rocks, the Bindi birds command the viewer's full attention with their presence, fine detailing, and subtle use of color.

NOTICE THE INTERPLAY EXPRESSED BY THE INTERTWINING OF THE HERONS' NECKS AND BEAKS. THE ARTIST'S APPRECIATION FOR HIS SUBJECT IS CLEARLY REFLECTED IN THE WAY IN WHICH THE HERONS' COURTSHIP RITUALS ARE REPRESENTED.

CAPODIMONTE COLLECTIBLES

VIRGILIO BINDI'S TRADEMARK.

FROM HIS PERCH ATOP AN OLD STUMP, THE "ROYAL OWL" SURVEYS HIS KINGDOM.
SCULPTED BY VIRGILIO BINDI,
THIS IS A FINE EXAMPLE OF THE ARTIST'S SKILL
IN CAPTURING THE DISTINCTIVE MARKINGS AND PLUMAGE.

CAPODIMONTE COLLECTIBLES

VIRGILIO BINDI'S HAUNTINGLY BEAUTIFUL "SNOW OWL" DEPICTS A SUBJECT
THAT HAS LONG BEEN A POPULAR ONE FOR BIRD ARTISTS.
A STUDENT OF TAY, WHO WAS ITALY'S MOST FAMOUS SCULPTOR OF BIRDS,
BINDI HAS CAPTURED THE VERY ESSENCE OF THIS RARE PREDATOR.

CAPODIMONTE COLLECTIBLES

THIS SMALL FIGURINE OF A PAIR
OF DUCKS IS FROM LUCIANO CAZZOLA'S
FOUR-PIECE SERIES OF SMALL
ANIMALS AND FOWL
FOR PORCELLANE PRINCIPE.
MADE OF PORCELAIN, THESE ANIMATED
FIGURES OF DUCKS ARE FINELY
DETAILED AND HAND-PAINTED.

THIS CHARMING PAIR OF GEESE IS
FROM CAZZOLA'S SERIES OF
SMALL ANIMALS AND FOWL
FOR PORCELLANE PRINCIPE.
NOTICE THE WAY IN WHICH CAZZOLA
HAS BROUGHT A SMALL CORNER
OF THE BARNYARD TO LIFE.
EVEN THE EARTH AND TUFTS OF
GRASS ADD TO THE AMBIENCE.

BEPI TAY, WHO WAS BORN GIUSEPPE TAGLIARIOL, WAS CONSIDERED A YOUNG PRODIGY.
SOON, SCULPTURES OF BIRDS BY THIS ITALIAN GENIUS
WERE COVETED BY DISCERNING COLLECTORS.
THIS PAIR OF MALLARD DUCKS, PRODUCED BY KAISER PORZELLAN, REVEALS TAY'S SKILL
IN CAPTURING WATERFOWL ABOUT TO TAKE FLIGHT.
OF SPECIAL NOTE ARE THE MARKINGS AND HUES OF THESE COLORFUL BIRDS.

CAPODIMONTE COLLECTIBLES

THE BALD EAGLE FASCINATED
SCULPTOR BEPI TAY;
AGAIN AND AGAIN HE
SCULPTED THIS REGAL SYMBOL
OF THE AMERICAN DREAM.
THIS TAY "JUBILEE EAGLE,"
PRODUCED BY
KAISER PORZELLAN, REVEALS
HIS ULTIMATE SUCCESS.
NOTHING IS MISSED BY THE
EAGLE'S PIERCING GLANCE,
AND HIS WINGS ARE
PARTIALLY EXTENDED AS IF
POISED FOR FLIGHT.

BEPI TAY REACHED THE ZENITH OF HIS CAREER WHEN THE UNITED STATES
WAS CELEBRATING ITS BICENTENNIAL.
HAVING FINALLY CAPTURED THE MAJESTIC POWER OF THE BALD EAGLE, TAY WAS
COMMISSIONED BY A NUMBER
OF NATIONS TO PRODUCE BALD EAGLE SCULPTURES AS GIFTS OF STATE
TO HONOR AMERICA'S BICENTENNIAL.
PRODUCED BY KAISER PORZELLAN, THESE EAGLES WERE AMONG HIS LAST COMMISSIONS.
TAY DIED A SHORT TIME LATER.

CAPODIMONTE COLLECTIBLES

WE ARE IMMEDIATELY DRAWN TO
THE EAGLE'S PIERCING EYES
AND THE UTILITARIAN
SHAPE OF HIS BEAK.
NOTE THAT THE FEATHERS
OF THE HEAD HAVE BEEN
HIGHLIGHTED TO REPLICATE
THE FEATHERS ON THE
WINGS AND BODY.

THIS PAINTED "EAGLE" FROM AURO BELCARI FOR DEAR
HAS A VISUAL COMPOSITION SIMILAR TO THAT OF
THE WHITE BISQUE "EAGLE" ON PAGE 155.
BY USING THE COLD-CAST PORCELAIN METHOD, THE ARTIST
HAS ACHIEVED THE EXTREMELY INTRICATE SURFACE NEEDED TO RECREATE
BOTH THE COLOR AND
TEXTURES OF THE EAGLE'S PLUMAGE.

CAPODIMONTE COLLECTIBLES

"FALCON," A SCULPTURE OF THE BIRD OF PREY HIGHLY PRIZED BY EUROPEAN ROYALTY, CAPTURES THE PIERCING VISION AND DISTINCTIVE MARKINGS OF THIS DEADLY SKY WARRIOR. SCULPTED BY ERMANNO FARINA FOR THE DEAR WILDLIFE SERIES, IT SHOWS COLD-CAST PORCELAIN'S ABILITY TO RETAIN FINE DETAILING. HAND-PAINTING TECHNIQUES FURTHER ENHANCE THIS ADVANTAGE. NOTICE THE WAY IN WHICH THE FALCON'S STANCE COMMANDS RESPECT, WHILE HIS SEEMINGLY ORDINARY MARKINGS CONCEAL HIS STEALTH AS A HUNTER.

CAPODIMONTE COLLECTIBLES

PERCHED ON A POST, THIS
BLUE AND GOLD PARROT
FLAPS HIS WINGS TO SHOW
THEIR STRENGTH AND GRACE.
THIS PARROT SCULPTURE
WAS DONE BY VIRGILIO BINDI,
ONE OF ITALY'S
MOST PROMINENT MASTERS.
NOTICE THE WAY IN WHICH
EACH LAYER OF FEATHERS HAS
BEEN DEFINED SO
DISTINCTIVELY WITHOUT
DETRACTING FROM THE OVERALL
APPEARANCE OF
TROPICAL BEAUTY.

CAPODIMONTE COLLECTIBLES

LIKE HIS MENTOR BEPI TAY, ERMANNO FARINA SEEMS ABLE TO EXPRESS
THE VERY SPIRIT OF HIS BIRD SUBJECTS
IN THIS GROUPING OF TWO WHITE DOVES OF
COLD-CAST PORCELAIN FROM DEAR.
BOTH THE ANATOMY AND PLUMAGE OF THESE LOVELY CREATURES
SHOW HIS MASTERFUL TECHNIQUE, AND HE HAS ADDED A BRANCH
AND A HANDFUL OF FLOWERS AS ACCENTS.

CAPODIMONTE COLLECTIBLES

IN ANTONIO BORSATO'S
"ALPINE REFUGE," A MOTHER BIRD
AND HER YOUNG BROOD
HAVE MADE THEMSELVES AT HOME
ATOP AN ALPINE
MOUNTAIN CLIMBER'S CAP.
BORSATO REVEALS BOTH THE
TATTERED STATE OF THEIR NEW
ABODE AND THE EXPECTATIONS
OF THESE NEWLY HATCHED BIRDS,
WHO CHIRP AND SING WHILE
TESTING THEIR SMALL WINGS.

"IF THE SHOE FITS" IS A WHIMSICAL
OFFERING FROM BORSATO.
THIS CHARMING PIECE
SHOWS A MOTHER BIRD FEEDING
HER BABY, WHO FOR SOME REASON
IS PERCHED ATOP
AN OLD LEATHER SHOE.
DESPITE THIS INCONGRUITY,
THE MOTHER'S DUTIES
GO ON UNINTERRUPTED.

CAPODIMONTE COLLECTIBLES

ERMANNO FARINA, WHO WAS A
STUDENT OF BEPI TAY, BRINGS
REALISM AND A NATURALNESS
OF MOVEMENT TO HIS BIRD
SCULPTURES. THIS "SNOWY OWL,"
FROM THE DEAR WILDLIFE
SERIES IN COLD-CAST
PORCELAIN, HAS A SHARP EYE
FOR HIS PREY, WHILE THE
SUBTLE SHADING OF HIS
FEATHERS PROVIDES HIM WITH
CONCEALMENT FROM BOTH HIS
ENEMIES AND HIS VICTIMS.
ALSO NOTE THE REALISM
OF THE ROCKY BASE,
COMPLETE WITH
SNOW AND MUSHROOMS.

A DUCK LEAVES THE SAFETY
OF THE MARSH FOR THE
UNKNOWN DANGERS OF
A HOSTILE WORLD.
IN "MALLARD," FROM DEAR'S
BISQUE WILDLIFE SERIES
IN COLD-CAST PORCELAIN,
AURO BELCARI HAS SKILLFULLY
GIVEN THE APPEARANCE
THAT THE MALLARD HAS BROKEN
FREE OF ITS SURROUNDINGS
AND IS SOARING
TO FREEDOM.
THE REALISM AND DETAILING
OF BOTH THE WING
FEATHERS AND THE MARSH
GRASSES MAKE THIS
AN INTERESTING PIECE.

THE MOST POPULAR FIGURINE IN THE DEAR LINE, THE "EAGLE," FROM AURO BELCARI'S WILDLIFE SERIES, CAPTURES THE ALMOST MYSTICAL APPEARANCE OF THIS SYMBOL OF THE AMERICAN SPIRIT. PRODUCED OF COLD-CAST PORCELAIN WITH A WHITE MATTE FINISH, IT SHOWS THE STRIKING BUT DIFFICULT IMAGE OF AN EAGLE POISED FOR FLIGHT. CLEARLY VISIBLE ARE THE BONE AND MUSCLE STRUCTURES AND THE COMPLEX COMBINATION OF FEATHERS NEEDED TO SEND THIS MAGNIFICENT BIRD SOARING UP TO THE HEAVENS. NOTICE THE PRECISION AND DETAILING NEEDED TO RECREATE THE MANY AND DIVERSE FEATHERS ON THE UNDERSIDE OF THE EAGLE'S WING.

CAPODIMONTE COLLECTIBLES

AMONGST THE MOST POPULAR CAPODIMONTE FLORAL PORCELAINS ARE
RENDITIONS OF ROSES.
ACCORDING TO MYTH, THE ROSE WAS WHITE AS SNOW UNTIL IT WAS BATHED
IN THE BLOOD OF VENUS, WHO WAS WOUNDED
GOING TO THE AID OF ADONIS.
THIS "MY LOVE ROSE" FROM NAPOLEON IS UNADORNED AND SURROUNDED
ONLY BY ROSE LEAVES AND A SINGLE BUD.

CAPODIMONTE COLLECTIBLES

FLOWERS

Capodimonte flowers were rumored to have been created because Charles VII, King of Naples, was allergic to the blossoms in the palace garden. It is an interesting bit of folklore. Actually, the kings of France and Germany were already enjoying elegant porcelain flowers, and Charles's cousin, Louis XIV, had decorated an entire room in one of his palaces with porcelain florals. These porcelains probably did more to spur Charles's interest than his sniffles and sneezes.

It is a dispute best left to art historians. Regardless of the origins of the porcelain flowers, Italians from all walks of life took them to their hearts. In response to universal outpourings of affection, the artists at Capodimonte created flowers and greenery of such beauty and color that the name Capodimonte has become synonymous with the concept of porcelain florals.

Flowers provided an intriguing challenge to the early Capodimonte artists. Most of the earliest examples reveal the artists' attempts to create somewhat plain, but perfect, replicas of such common garden flowers as roses and primroses. The flourishing trade Europe had with China and the Middle East helped introduce exotic new flowers to the imagination of European artists.

The mysterious tulip from Persia and the cherry blossoms of the Orient were a heady stimulant. The competition among artists to incorporate these new wonders into the works they presented to their royal patrons became so intense that floral artists began fashioning exotic blossoms that were a blend of both real and imagined flowers. These lush new hybrids that neither wilted nor faded outshone even the most perfect natural flowers.

THIS HOLLY POINSETTIA BRANCH FROM NAPOLEON IS A FINE EXAMPLE OF AN IMAGINATIVE COMBINATION OF CONTRASTING ELEMENTS. SMOOTH ROUND STONES AND A WOOD SCULPTURE PROVIDE THE PERFECT BACKGROUND FOR THE JAGGED SCARLET POINSETTIA PETALS. EACH OF THE PERFECTLY FORMED PETALS IS CAREFULLY ETCHED WITH THE MARKINGS OF THIS TROPICAL BEAUTY. THE GOLDEN STAMEN AND PISTIL AND HOLLY BERRIES PROVIDE PERFECT ACCENTS FOR THIS HOLIDAY FAVORITE.

The response to the artists's florals was overwhelming. Charles was so enthusiastic that he immediately commissioned his staff to begin work on the first of three porcelain rooms to be built during his reign. Decorated with thousands of clusters of flowers, fruits, foliage, and vines, the porcelain room at Portici ensured forever the reputation of Capodimonte porcelains.

A TINY, DELICATELY FASHIONED BASKET WITH A BOW HANDLE IS FILLED WITH MINIATURE ROSES AND BUDS. THIS CAREFULLY FASHIONED PORCELAIN MINIATURE IS A TREASURE FOR COLLECTORS WHO ENJOY THE CAPODIMONTE STYLE BUT DON'T HAVE ROOM FOR THE LARGER PIECES.

Great skill and patience was needed to produce the thousands of teardrop-sized petals used in creating a single blossom, and the talented artists and artisans were well rewarded by the Crown. By definition, Capodimonte florals are still handmade of fine porcelain in Italy, where each flower is assembled and painted by hand. The more intricate or complex a floral piece is, the greater its value.

The closing of the Capodimonte factories in the early 1800s did not diminish interest in the stylized Capodimonte floral porcelains. The once-prized techniques for creating these lush, almost overpowering florals were spread throughout the country by the artists and painters who now plied their trade in small, privately owned porcelain factories.

Lacking the resources of royalty, these factories could not afford the experimentation needed to achieve the proper formulas or to buy the costly, but essential, ingredients for high-quality porcelain. The execution of a piece might be masterful, but the porcelain was frequently brittle or soft and cracked easily.

In spite of this deficiency, floral groupings have remained extremely popular down through the centuries. These fragile but elegant pieces have always been purchased by tourists attempting to take home a small reminder of the beauty of the Italian countryside. And many immigrants seeking a better life in the New World carefully packed their porcelain treasures to remind them of the culture they were leaving behind. Once these same immigrants had made their fortunes, they decorated their homes with all manner of art and decorative accessories imported from their homeland.

Because of the early problems with breakage, it was not unusual to find large and complex arrangements with chipped or broken petals. Few people were willing to part with their still-prized treasures, and more than one owner concealed the damage by displaying the florals in a shadowy corner or by simply turning the piece each time a leaf or petal was lost.

Although the very early florals had been surprisingly natural and unadorned, later examples gradually became more stylized and elaborate. New combinations of paint and glazes frequently gave the florals a shiny appearance. A few rustic baskets were used as containers, but gradually most of the containers and accessories became increasingly elaborate, almost rococo in appearance.

THIS TINY, EXQUISITELY FASHIONED WHITE BASKET FROM NAPOLEON, FILLED WITH AN ASSORTMENT OF GREENERY AND FLOWERS, IS A FINE EXAMPLE OF THE CAPODIMONTE FLORAL STYLE. THE ARRANGEMENT IS ONLY THREE INCHES TALL. THE HANDWOVEN PORCELAIN BASKET IS DECORATED WITH A TWISTED HANDLE, AND THE DELICATE BOUQUET WAS MADE AND PAINTED BY HAND.

Containers made of twisted or braided strands of snow-white porcelain trimmed with gold remain one the most popular means of presenting florals. These twisted white strands of porcelain are repeated in baskets, elaborate vases, bird cages, carts, and all kinds of containers.

The life-styles and tastes of later generations found little beauty in these elaborate decorative styles and sought simpler, more natural floral pieces. In the past ten to twenty years, an entirely new genre of Capodimonte florals has begun to appear. The realism of these floral offerings of today is more reminiscent of the earliest Capodimonte flowers. Current Capodimonte florals from the artists of Brando and Napoleon are both realistic and surprisingly simple in arrangement.

Although the first florals were called simply a red or yellow mum, many of the current offerings are replicas of specific varieties. Porcelain orchids, poinsettias, camellias, lilies, tulips, and hibiscus can now be everlasting reminders of nature's originals. The Napoleon line is of interest because for the first time it makes available accurate replicas of patented rose varieties such as "Peace," "Queen Elizabeth," and "Tropicana."

THE VIBRANT, GOLDEN TRUMPETS
IN THIS DAFFODIL GROUPING
FROM NAPOLEON PROCLAIM
THE ARRIVAL OF SPRING.
GREEK MYTHS SAY THAT
PERSEPHONE WAS GATHERING
NARCISSI WHEN SHE WAS
CARRIED OFF BY PLUTO.
THE DAFFODIL OR NARCISSUS
IS CALLED THE FLOWER
OF THE UNDERWORLD BECAUSE
OF ITS MEDICINAL PROPERTIES
AND ITS PALLID LUNAR
APPEARANCE.

CAPODIMONTE COLLECTIBLES

JUST AS THE RAYS OF SUNLIGHT
GRADUALLY COLOR THE MORNING
SKY, EACH PETAL OF THE
ORANGISH-PINK "TYPHOON ROSE"
BY NAPOLEON REVEALS THE
SUBTLE BLUSH OF COLOR
RADIATING OUT TO THE EDGE
OF EACH PETAL.
TWO PERFECTLY FORMED ROSES
AND A PARTIALLY OPENED
BUD COMPLETE THIS
EXQUISITE GROUPING.

CAPODIMONTE COLLECTIBLES

THIS FLORAL FIGURINE IS FROM ARNART'S FOUR-PIECE DOUBLE-TULIP COLLECTION IN THEIR "N" CAPODIMONTE COLLECTION. MADE OF FINE BISQUE PORCELAIN, THIS TULIP GROUPING IS UNUSUAL BECAUSE WE ARE UNACCUSTOMED TO SEEING TULIPS RESTING ON THEIR SIDES. THESE TULIPS ARE MORE STYLIZED THAN REALISTIC.

THIS DELICATE PORCELAIN ROSE FLORAL FROM ARNART'S "N" CAPODIMONTE COLLECTION, SHOWING A NOSEGAY OF A HALF DOZEN FRESH PALE PINK ROSES AND THEIR ACCOMPANYING ROSEBUDS AND GREENERY, HAS AN AMBIENCE THAT CONTRIBUTES TO ITS ROMANTIC APPEAL.

A SYMBOL OF MATURE BEAUTY,
THE ORCHID'S IRREGULAR
PETALS WITH RUFFLED
EDGES SEEM TO HAVE BEEN
DIPPED IN LAVENDER.
THIS BISQUE PORCELAIN
ORCHID IS ONE OF THE FOUR
ORCHID BLOSSOMS IN THE
ORCHID SERIES FROM
ARNART'S "N" CAPODIMONTE
COLLECTION.

THIS ROSE CENTERPIECE BASKET,
IN BISQUE PORCELAIN
FROM ARNART'S "N" CAPODIMONTE
COLLECTION, CONTAINS FOUR
FULL-BLOWN ROSES SURROUNDED
BY BUDS AND FOLIAGE.
THIS PIECE IS PARTICULARLY
STRIKING BECAUSE OF THE
CONTRAST BETWEEN A SINGLE
RED ROSE AND THE PINK
ROSES AND BUDS.

CAPODIMONTE COLLECTIBLES

THE BRILLIANT ORANGE CORN POPPY ACCENTED WITH A VELVETY BLACK STAMEN
AND A BUTTON-SHAPED PISTIL IS COMMON THROUGHOUT
ASIA, EUROPE, AND AMERICA.
NAPOLEON CREATES THIS GROUPING WITH A Z-SHAPED BRANCH
AS A BACKDROP.
FOUR POPPIES IN FULL BLOOM ARE ARRANGED IN
AN ASYMMETRICAL ARRANGEMENT ACCENTED BY THE SOFT JAGGED
LEAVES OF THE POPPY.

CAPODIMONTE COLLECTIBLES

THIS GRACEFUL PINK CAMELLIA JAPONICA COMPOSITION BY NAPOLEON
COMBINES THE NATURAL CURVES OF BRANCH AND BLOSSOMS
AS THE BACKDROP FOR A SINGLE CREAMY PINK CAMELLIA.
GROWN FOR CENTURIES IN CHINA, THE FAINTLY SCENTED BLOSSOMS
RANGE FROM A CREAMY WHITE TO PINK AND RED.
LEGEND HAS IT THAT VENUS DEPRIVED THIS LOVELY FLOWER OF
ITS PERFUME BECAUSE IT FAILED TO INJURE CUPID,
WHO WAS DISOBEDIENT.

CAPODIMONTE COLLECTIBLES

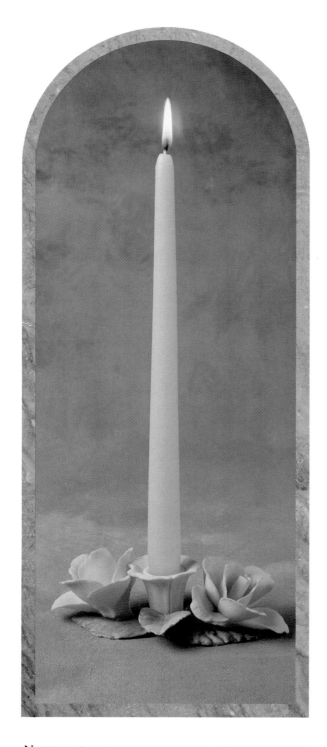

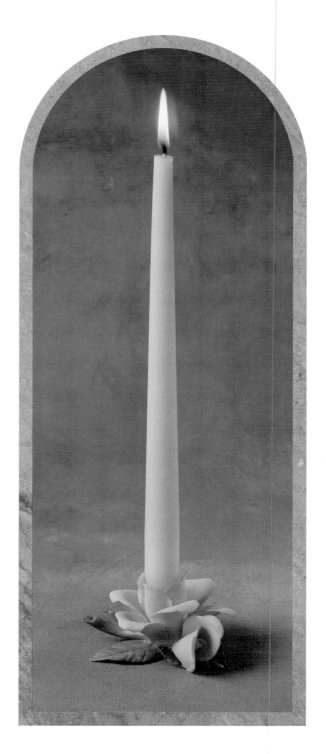

NAPOLEON'S CANDLESTICK DECORATED WITH TWO YELLOW
ROSEBUDS HAS A GENTLY FLUTED DESIGN.
NOTICE THE WAY IN WHICH THE BLOSSOMS ARE ARRANGED
SO THEY CAN BE ENJOYED
FROM ALL ANGLES.

THE PETALS OF THIS PINK ROSEBUD FROM NAPOLEON
CONTAIN A CANDLE HOLDER TO ADD A FLOWERY
TOUCH TO A TABLE SETTING.
ROSE LEAVES AND THE PARTIALLY OPENED
ROSE PETALS GIVE THIS PIECE
AN UNEXPECTED GRACE.

PANSIES HAVE LONG BEEN INVITED TO TEA PARTIES BY
CHILDREN WHO ENJOYED THEIR TINY FACES.
NAPOLEON'S THREE-PANSY GROUPING REVEALS THE
SYMMETRY OF THE PANSY'S
FIVE DELICATELY MARKED PETALS.

THE PETALS OF THIS VIOLET CATTLEYA ORCHID FROM
NAPOLEON ARE GENTLY TOUCHED WITH GRADUAL
PROGRESSIONS OF SHADES OF VIOLET. THE VERY HEART
OF THE ORCHID IS BRUSHED WITH YELLOW EXTENDING TO
THE PETALS' PURPLE-TIPPED EDGES.

THIS FULL PINK ROSEBUD AND BLOSSOM FROM NAPOLEON
IS ENTIRELY HANDMADE.
EACH PETAL RECREATES THE SHAPE, TEXTURE,
AND MATTE FINISH OF FRESH ROSE PETALS.
THE THORNY STEM AND LEAVES ADD A NOTE OF REALISM.

EACH OF THESE VELVETY PETALS CAPTURES ALL THE
SUBTLE SHADES OF YELLOW IN NAPOLEON'S
SPRING ROSE BUD.
THE CALYX, THE SMALL GREEN LEAVES, STILL PROTECTS
THE YET UNOPENED BUD.

THE SWAN HOLDS A UNIQUE
PLACE IN ITALIAN ART.
THIS GENTLE BIRD'S GRACE
AND SNOW-WHITE PLUMAGE
HAVE BEEN CAPTURED
IN CERAMIC.
A NOSEGAY OF PINK ROSES
AND WHITE BLOSSOMS HAS
BEEN PLACED UPON
THE SWAN'S SNOWY BACK.

THE BASE FOR THIS CERAMIC
CENTERPIECE OF PINK ROSES
IS UNUSUALLY SHALLOW
AND IS GLAZED
TO ACHIEVE A RICHER,
MORE SUBDUED APPEARANCE.

CAPODIMONTE COLLECTIBLES

THIS CERAMIC GROUPING OF
A FLAT BASKET FILLED
WITH A VARIETY OF
BLOSSOMS IS THE KIND
OF ARRANGEMENT THAT MOST
PEOPLE ASSOCIATE
WITH THE NAME
CAPODIMONTE.
NO ATTEMPT HAS BEEN MADE
TO CREATE EXACT REPLICAS
OF REAL FLOWERS.
INSTEAD, THESE BLOSSOMS
HAVE A LUSH, ROMANTIC,
ALMOST CAREFREE
APPEARANCE.

THIS CERAMIC BASKET IS
FILLED WITH STEMMED CHERRIES
AND GLOSSY GREEN LEAVES.
IT IS SMALL ENOUGH FOR
A CURIO CABINET OR FOR
AN ACCENT AT
A PLACE SETTING.

CAPODIMONTE COLLECTIBLES

EACH PETAL OF THESE DELICATE
WHITE BLOSSOMS
RECREATES THE SHAPE OF
THE BLOOM AND THE GENTLE
TUCK IN THE HEART
WHERE BOTH THE STAMEN AND
THE PISTIL REIGN.
ALSO NOTE THE WAXY GREEN
LEAVES OF THESE
DELICATE BLOSSOMS.

THIS SEEMINGLY SIMPLE GROUPING,
"CHANNELLE ROSE COMPOSITION" FROM NAPOLEON,
COMBINES THORNY ROSEBUDS IN VARYING STAGES OF
DEVELOPMENT WITH EACH PALE GOLD PETAL
GENTLY TOUCHED WITH SOFT BLUSHES OF PINK.
A HANDFUL OF DELICATE WHITE BLOSSOMS AND BUDS
PROVIDE AN UNUSUAL ACCENT.

CAPODIMONTE COLLECTIBLES

THIS OBLONG CERAMIC BASKET
IS A ROMANTIC REMINDER
OF AN OLD-FASHIONED
GARDEN, WHERE BASKETS WITH
THESE HIGH, BRAIDED
HANDLES WERE USED WHILE
PICKING FLOWERS.
HIGHLIGHTED WITH UMBER TINTS,
THIS BASKET IS DECORATED
WITH HAND-FASHIONED
CERAMIC FLOWERS.

THE VELVETY-PETALED HIBISCUS HAS BECOME THE FLORAL EMBLEM OF HAWAII
AND IS A MEMBER OF THE MALLOW FAMILY.
THIS HIBISCUS GROUPING FROM NAPOLEON DEPICTS THE DELICATELY
TINTED BLOSSOMS WITH GOLDEN STAMEN AND
PISTILS IN THE CENTER.
THE NOTCHED WAXY-GREEN AND WOODY BRANCHES OFFER A PLEASING
CONTRAST TO THESE EXQUISITE BLOSSOMS.

FLORAL OFFERINGS LIKE THIS
CERAMIC GILT-TRIMMED BOWL
FILLED WITH A MIXED
BOUQUET OF FLOWERS WERE
HIGHLY PRIZED AND
FREQUENTLY GIVEN AS
WEDDING GIFTS.
THEY WERE ALWAYS GIVEN
A PLACE OF HONOR
IN THE HOME.
IF A PETAL WAS LOST,
THE PIECE WAS SIMPLY
TURNED TO MAKE THE LOSS
LESS CONSPICUOUS.

A CERAMIC WOVEN BASKET
PAINTED CHALK-WHITE PROVIDES
A STRIKING CONTAINER FOR
A MIXED BOUQUET.
ALTHOUGH THE PATTERN OF
THE BASKET'S WOVEN
SIDES IS CONVENTIONAL,
THE LOW, OBLONG SHAPE OF
THIS BASKET IS UNUSUAL.
NOTICE THE OPENNESS
AND CASUAL ARRANGEMENTS
OF THESE MULTICOLORED
BLOSSOMS.

THIS FOOTED CENTERPIECE OF
MILK-WHITE CERAMIC IS
FILLED WITH A MEDLEY OF
CHERRIES, BANANAS, ORANGES,
LEMONS, AND PEARS.
THE PLUMP, SUCCULENT
CHERRIES AND THE ROSY BLUSH
ON THE PEARS ARE
CERAMIC, TOO.
THE TANTALIZING BEAUTY
OF THESE FRUITS IS MEANT
ONLY FOR THE EYE.

THIN ROPES OF PURE WHITE
CERAMIC HAVE BEEN
WOVEN INTO AN UNUSUAL
DESIGN FOR THIS BASKET
FILLED WITH FRUIT.
NOTICE THE DOUBLE TWISTS
USED AS A HANDLE.

CAPODIMONTE COLLECTIBLES

THIS ORNATE CERAMIC AFTER-DINNER COFFEE SET
IS ENTIRELY HAND-PAINTED.
THE BRASS-HANDLED TRAY HOLDS
A COVERED SUGAR BOWL AND SIX CUPS AND SAUCERS.
THIS TYPE OF SET WAS QUITE POPULAR DURING THE REIGNS
OF BOTH KING CHARLES AND KING FERDINAND.
NOTICE THE SIMPLE GOLD RIM ON THE TRAY
AND THE UNUSUAL DESIGN ON EACH CUP.

CAPODIMONTE COLLECTIBLES

174

DECORATIVE
ACCESSORIES

Among the first items produced by the royal porcelain factories were tableware, vases, and small decorated boxes. Following the lead of the porcelain makers in Germany and France, the modelers and artists in King Charles's factory were soon producing elaborate tea, coffee, and chocolate services.

The shapes and handles of the early porcelains show a baroque influence. But instead of the bas-relief that adorned some of the earliest works, the dinner services, wine pitchers, and tea, coffee, and chocolate services were decorated with hand-painted drawings similiar to the art being used on English and German porcelains.

The more practical services were then followed by such items as covered candy dishes, soup tureens, and all sorts of covered bowls. Many of the open bowls were also used as containers for floral arrangements.

Today, Capodimonte florals are frequently freestanding floral centerpieces for the table and are often accompanied by matching candlesticks. In addition to the freestanding porcelains, many of these floral room accessories are displayed in urns and gleaming white ribbon baskets or the more rustic woven baskets. Although the symbolism is unclear, swans are also used to hold elegant floral groupings.

The completion of the porcelain room at King Charles's summer palace at Portici probably did more to promote the use of Capodimonte porcelains as a decorative tool than any other event. The powder and trinket boxes that were on milady's dressing table were joined by mirrors, perfume bottles, and even a pitcher and basin in the Capodimonte style. Through the years, complete pieces of furniture—washstands, end tables, desks, and even tea carts—have been made and decorated with porcelain.

Most of the European immigrants who came to America were accompanied only by their dreams. But once they managed to get beyond the everyday struggle for survival, they began purchasing the highly ornate porcelains and ceramics that reminded them of the richness of their European heritage. An elaborately decorated mirror and console, or a pedestal with an arrangement of flowers or a figurine, lent the appearance of substance and culture.

These large decorative pieces show a real competition between swirling baroque fashions and the more natural style represented by the use of vinelike handles. Ironically, the ornamentation on these vases, planters, and urns frequently upstage their contents.

Elegant chandeliers, lamps, candelabras, and candlesticks have been immensely popular. Chandeliers can be gilded or decorated with glass leaves and garlands of flowers. Although less ornate, the candelabras also are gilded and have floral decorative art. There are ceiling and wall light fixtures and even light-switch plates decorated in the Capodimonte style.

Lamp bases feature figurines from the royal court or a rural setting. These lamps, which appear quaint by today's standards, come with round globes decorated with flowers or silk shades trimmed with fringe.

THIS HAND-PAINTED CERAMIC
CRUET SET FEATURES
A STAND DECORATED WITH AN
ATTRACTIVE DESIGN
AROUND THE BASE.
EACH OF THE CRUETS
IS HIGHLIGHTED WITH GOLD.

SIX CUPS AND SAUCERS,
A COVERED SUGAR BOWL, AND
A BRASS-HANDLED SERVING TRAY
MAKE UP THIS MOCHA SET.
NOTICE THE GOLDEN APPEARANCE
ON THE INSIDE OF EACH CUP
AND THE HAND-PAINTED
PASTORAL SCENES USED
TO DECORATE ALL THE PIECES.

CAPODIMONTE COLLECTIBLES

177

THE SHAPE OF THIS CERAMIC CLOCK CASE IS
REMINISCENT OF COURTLY ELEGANCE.
THE CLOCK IS DECORATED WITH FLOWERS AND
HIGHLIGHTED WITH GOLD.

THIS SMALL PORCELAIN CANDY DISH HAS A LID DECORATED
WITH A NOSEGAY OF PINK ROSEBUDS.
THE FINAL TOUCH IS A SIMPLE GOLD BAND
ON THE RIM OF THE LID.

A TRIANGLE OF CANDLES ON THE LOWER LEVEL
SURROUNDS A FOURTH, SOMEWHAT HIGHER CANDLE IN
THIS ORNATE CERAMIC CANDELABRA.
A DECORATIVE DESIGN CONNECTS THE TRIANGLE.
IN SPITE OF THE INTRICATE DESIGN,
ROSEBUDS ARE USED FOR A LAVISH TOUCH OF COLOR.

CAPODIMONTE COLLECTIBLES

THIS HIGHLY DECORATED CERAMIC PITCHER HAS AN
ORNATE HANDLE AND UNUSUAL RIDGES ON THE SPOUT.
THE ENTIRE PIECE WAS HIGHLIGHTED WITH UMBER
TONES BEFORE THE ROSES AND BUDS WERE ADDED.

THE DESIGN ON THE BASE OF THIS LOW
CERAMIC CANDELABRA IS HIGHLIGHTED WITH
GOLD AND DECORATED WITH
SINGLE ROSEBUDS ON THE BASE
AND IN THE CENTER.

BOTH THE CERAMIC PERFUME BOTTLE AND THE
MATCHING JEWELRY BOX HAVE A FOOTED DESIGN.
NOTICE THE EMBOSSED PATTERN ON THE SIDES AND
THE FLORAL ACCENTS ON EACH ITEM.

CAPODIMONTE COLLECTIBLES

THIS ELABORATE TWELVE-LIGHT CHANDELIER IS CURRENTLY THE MOST POPULAR CAPODIMONTE CHANDELIER BEING MADE. EACH OF THE GRACEFULLY CURVED CERAMIC ARMS IS EMBOSSED WITH BAROQUE CURVES HIGHLIGHTED WITH GOLD.

BOTTOM, LEFT: ATOP EACH OF THE ARMS IS A SCALLOPED BASE THAT HOLDS ANOTHER FLUTED BASE FOR EACH LIGHT BULB.

BOTTOM, RIGHT: SMALL BRASS RINGS HOLD THE HAND-FASHIONED ROSES THAT HANG DOWN FROM EACH ARM.

CAPODIMONTE COLLECTIBLES

TOP, LEFT:
THIS CERAMIC LAMP HAS
AS ITS BASE A FIGURE OF
A MAN HOLDING A MASK.
MANY LAMPS ARE AVAILABLE
EITHER WITH GLOBE SHADES OR
WITH FABRIC SHADES,
WHICH ARE MORE POPULAR
IN AMERICA.

TOP, RIGHT:
THE BASE OF THIS LAMP IS
A CERAMIC FIGURINE OF A GIRL
WITH A BASKET OF FLOWERS,
AN EXAMPLE OF THE
ROMANTIC PASTORAL THEME.

BOTTOM, LEFT:
THIS LAMP FROM THE ARMANI LAMP
COLLECTION FEATURES GIUSEPPE
ARMANI'S FIGURINE "ON TOES,"
A YOUNG BALLERINA CAPTURED IN A
DRAMATIC ARABESQUE.
IT IS PRODUCED BY FLORENCE
SCULTURE D'ARTE OF COLD-CAST
PORCELAIN. SPECIAL CARE IN
THE HAND-PAINTING ACHIEVES THE
RIGHT FACIAL EXPRESSION.

BOTTOM, RIGHT:
THIS CERAMIC LAMP SHOWING
A COUPLE ON A SWING IS MEANT TO
CAPTURE THE GAY ABANDON OF
YOUNG LOVERS ENJOYING
SIMPLE PLEASURES.

GARLANDS OF FLOWERS AND
EMBOSSED BAROQUE CURVES AND
SCALLOPS DECORATE THIS ORNATE
CERAMIC CHANDELIER.
NOTICE THE USE OF SINGLE
ROSEBUDS ATTACHED TO EACH OF
THE FIVE GLOBES.

BOTTOM, LEFT:
THE BASE OF THIS LAMP
FEATURES A PAIR OF
SPANISH DANCERS IN THE MIDST
OF AN ANIMATED ROUTINE.
MADE OF CERAMIC,
THIS LAMP FEATURES A GLOBE
DECORATED WITH CLUSTERS
OF SMALL FLOWERS.

BOTTOM, RIGHT:
THIS GLOBE LAMP FEATURES
A CERAMIC FIGURE IN
THE CAPODIMONTE STYLE.
THE BOY WITH A FLOWER BASKET
HAS AN ANIMATED
APPEARANCE AND A PLEASANT
FACIAL EXPRESSION.

THIS CERAMIC END TABLE IS ONE OF THE PIECES OF FURNITURE THAT INCORPORATE THE STYLE OF FURNITURE USED DURING THE EARLY CAPODIMONTE PERIOD AS WELL AS THE DECORATIVE FLORAL TOUCHES THAT WERE POPULAR. NOTICE THE BAROQUE CURVES AND SCROLLS, THE GARLAND OF HAND-FASHIONED FLOWERS ON THE BASE, AND THE FLORAL DESIGN ON THE TABLE TOP.

BOTTOM, LEFT:
CAPODIMONTE SWITCH PLATES, WHICH ADD A DISTINCTIVE TOUCH TO ROOMS DECORATED IN A FORMAL OR ORNATE MANNER, ARE AN EXTREMELY POPULAR ITEM.

BOTTOM, RIGHT:
THIS CERAMIC OVAL MIRROR INCORPORATES BOTH THE OPULENCE OF THE BAROQUE ART AND THE ROMANTIC AMBIENCE OF THE GARLAND OF ROSES CIRCLING THE FRAME. SMALL BOUQUETS OF PINK ROSES ACCENT THE TOP AND BOTTOM OF THE MIRROR.

CAPODIMONTE COLLECTIBLES

183

A FIGURINE LIKE "MARIKA," BY LUCIANO CAZZOLA FOR PORCELLANE PRINCIPE,
IS THE RESULT OF PATIENT, PAINSTAKING WORK.
THE INDIVIDUAL PARTS MUST BE MOLDED AND CAREFULLY ASSEMBLED.
THE PAINTERS GIVE A ROSY BLUSH TO MARIKA'S CHEEKS AND
TO THE HUNDREDS OF ROSES IN HER WHEELBARROW
BEFORE THIS HANDSOME FIGURINE IS FIRED.

CAPODIMONTE COLLECTIBLES

THE ART OF
MAKING PORCELAIN

Porcelain's early history is shrouded in mystery; the first allusions to porcelain, or "white gold," appear in China around 1320 B.C. No legends or folk tales suggest who was the first to discover that simple clays could be transformed into translucent porcelain.

It was Marco Polo who introduced the first fragile pieces of porcelain to European kings and bishops. Merchant travelers were quickly dispatched to China to bring back more of this exquisite material. Polite requests were made for information on the processes used in making porcelain, but the Chinese demurely refused to reveal their trade secrets.

Europeans might have been forced to submit to China's monopoly on the porcelain market had it not been for Johann Friedrick Böttger, who serendipitously discovered the formula for porcelain. A German alchemist, Böttger had been searching for a formula for turning base metals into gold. Though his gold experiments were a failure, all was not lost; in 1709, his failed experiments yielded the first European porcelain.

The following year, the porcelain works at Meissen, Germany, was established, and within the next decade porcelain factories sprang up all over Europe. The demand for the right clays and other raw materials needed in the process triggered extensive searches by workers throughout Europe. The wealth and status associated with porcelain production was quickly apparent. It's not surprising that Charles VII, King of Naples, entered the porcelain business shortly after his marriage to the granddaughter of the founder of the Meissen porcelain factory.

The process of producing high-quality porcelain has changed very little over the centuries. Electric kilns and better modeling materials have been developed, but the actual process remains an art dependent on the artisans who make the critical decisions throughout the process.

Making porcelain begins with an original sculpture created for the project. After consultations between artist and modelers, the final touches are added to the sculpture. It is then dissected into a number of sections. Plaster is poured around each of these dissected sections. The result is a series of plaster or waste molds.

These waste molds (negatives) are then used to make the block or case molds (the positive, or mother forms) of the original sculptured piece. The case molds are made of an extremely hard substance. All of the subsequent working molds, which are made of plaster, are taken from these case or positive molds. In order to preserve the fine detailing of the original sculpture, a working mold is used only 20 or 30 times before being discarded.

Because the materials and processes used in making the liquid porcelain, or slip, determine the quality, the transparency, and even the color of the porcelain, they are closely guarded secrets. The slip, which is usually the thickness of rich cream, is carefully poured into a working mold. When the mold master determines that the proper thickness of slip now covers the entire interior surface, the excess slip is poured off. The liquid remaining in the slip is quickly absorbed by the plaster, leaving a shell of porcelain within the mold.

The porcelain shell is then carefully removed from the mold and allowed to air-dry. At this stage, the porcelain is as fragile as a pie crust and must be handled with great care. The porcelain sections of the figurine are then assembled, using *barbottina,* or porcelain glue, and

PLASTER IS POURED AROUND
INDIVIDUAL SECTIONS OF THE FIGURINE
TO FORM THE PLASTER OR
WASTE MOLDS.

LIQUID SLIP IS POURED INTO
WORKING MOLDS.

INDIVIDUAL SECTIONS OF
THE FIGURINE ARE REMOVED FROM THEIR
WORKING MOLDS.

THE INDIVIDUAL SECTIONS ARE
CAREFULLY REASSEMBLED, AND ALL THE
JOINTS ARE SANDED TO
ERASE ALL LINES.

INDIVIDUAL FLOWERS ARE FASHIONED
BY HAND BEFORE BEING ATTACHED
TO THE FIGURINE.

CAPODIMONTE COLLECTIBLES

TO PREVENT ANY DISTORTION
OF THE FIGURINE'S ARM DURING THE
FIRING PROCESS, A PROP IS
PLACED UNDER THE ELBOW.

PARTIALLY ASSEMBLED,
AIR-DRIED PORCELAINS GO INTO
THE KILN TO BE FIRED AT
EXTREMELY HIGH TEMPERATURES.

REASSEMBLED SECTIONS ARE
HAND-PAINTED IN
A SERIES OF DECORATING AND
FIRING STAGES.

PARTIALLY PAINTED FIGURINES ARE
RETURNED TO THE KILN TO
SPEED UP THE DRYING PROCESS AND
TO HARDEN THE FINISH.

GOLD HIGHLIGHTS ARE ADDED
TO THE BASE OF THE FIGURINE AS
THE FINAL STEP IN THE
DECORATING PROCESS.

sanded to remove seam lines. Fine details, such as a bouquet of flowers, are assembled by hand and then added.

The assembled piece is then placed in the kiln, with supports to prevent breakage, and given its first firing. The heat evaporates the liquid in the slip, leaving a hard porcelain shell that has been reduced in size by about ten percent. The temperature in the kiln and the length of the firing period are critical elements at this stage in the process. A miscalculation in temperature, or excess moisture trapped within a piece, can result in a chain-reaction explosion within the kiln that can destroy weeks or months of work.

Each porcelain piece is then carefully hand-painted and fired. Because various minerals and oils used in the painting process liquefy at different temperatures, painting and firing are done in stages at different firing temperatures. When the painting process is completed, a final glaze is added to protect and highlight the surface.

Once the final firing is completed, all defective pieces are destroyed. For perfect pieces, the name of the piece, its edition size, the individual number of each piece, and the company's name or logo is added to the base. Porcelains are then carefully packed and shipped to distributors.

In the case of porcelains with a matte finish, the number of firings is limited. The porcelain is fired to achieve its translucent appearance. Florals that have a soft matte finish are then painted, but they are never fired after they are decorated. For this reason, these florals should never be immersed in water.

Some Capodimonte collectibles are not made of true hard-paste porcelain, but of a soft-paste product that is called ceramic. The formula is slightly different from that of porcelain, and it is fired at a much lower temperature. The material does not become vitrified in firing. Instead, varnish is applied and the piece is fired again. Ceramic figurines are

LUCIANO CAZZOLA HAS COMBINED
A NUMBER OF
INTERESTING ELEMENTS IN
"GIRL AT THE POOL," PRODUCED
BY PORCELLANE PRINCIPE.
A PRETTY YOUNG GIRL,
CARRYING A BOUQUET OF FLOWERS,
IS DAYDREAMING BESIDE A POOL,
WHILE A SNOW-WHITE GOOSE
LOOKS INQUISITIVELY
UP INTO HER FACE.

THESE ARE THE FRESHLY MOLDED SECTIONS
NEEDED TO COMPLETE THE FIGURINE
"GIRL AT THE POOL."
IN ADDITION TO THE BASE, THERE
ARE SECTIONS FOR THE HEAD AND TORSO,
THE GOOSE, THE BASKET, AND
THE BASKET HANDLE.

CAPODIMONTE COLLECTIBLES

more fragile than porcelain ones; a piece of metal will scratch the surface of ceramic, but it will not mark the surface of porcelain.

Artists' searches for new mediums and materials are as traditional as their urge to create meaningful works of art. Because of the considerable risk of breakage involved at every stage of porcelain production, the price of quality porcelain is frequently out of the reach of many collectors. A number of new materials are now being used instead of porcelain. The argument that swirls around the use of these materials is particularly heated amongst Capodimonte producers, because the traditional Capodimonte-style pieces are being produced by a number of companies that are using materials other than porcelain.

In recent years, a number of producers, such as Florence Sculture d'Arte, Giuseppe Armani, and the DEAR studio, have turned to a new material called "cold-cast porcelain." The main material in cold-cast porcelain is kaolin, which is a fine white clay that is an essential ingredient in all porcelain. The kaolin is mixed with synthetic resins to form the slip. Using many of the same techniques employed in the porcelain process, the resin slip is poured into the molds and high pressure is applied. The material hardens naturally, without the use of a kiln. The molds are then opened, and rough edges and marks left by the molds are finished by hand to eliminate all flaws. Each figurine is then hand-decorated.

In porcelain manufacture, much detail is lost through repeated firings in the kiln. Since the cold-cast porcelain is not subjected to the kiln's high temperatures, finer detailing can be achieved with this method. In addition, fewer pieces are lost in breakage, which means that the cost of these pieces can be kept within the range of many people who cannot afford the fine pieces produced in porcelain.

ball clay: a fine dark clay that turns white when fired.

baroque: a style of art and architecture developed in Europe between 1550 and 1700. It is typified by elaborate and ornate scrolls, curves, and other symmetrical ornamentation.

bas relief: a sculptural design that projects out from the background. This effect may be achieved through the use of a sculptural design that is a part of the primary mold. Slip poured into these molds recreates both the flat background and the raised decorative design. In other cases, a preformed design or figure is simply attached to the flat surface of a plate, figurine, or other blank piece.

biscuit: a fired ware, also called bisque, that has neither a glaze nor enamel applied to it. It may be either white or colored. Biscuit ware, or bisque, gets its name from its biscuit-like, matte texture.

case mold: a positive detailed replica, made of an extremely hard material, of an original section of a figurine. All future molds are taken from this case mold. The case mold is also referred to as a positive or mother form.

ceramic: a generic term frequently used for a piece that is made of some form of clay and is finished by firing at high temperatures. The term "ceramic" is being used by a few producers of Capodimonte collectibles to describe their soft-paste product lines. In order to achieve the desired results, minor changes are made in the formula and a significantly lower temperature is used during the firing process than is used for porcelain.

china: a term that originally referred to all porcelain ware coming from the nation of China. It is made of kaolin clay, feldspar, and quartz, and it must be fired at high temperatures to achieve its hardness or gloss. The term china is frequently used interchangeably with the term porcelain.

cold-cast porcelain: a relatively modern technique that combines kaolin powder with resin binders, which are then forced into a mold or die under great pressure to complete the forging process. This process does not require firing. The entire piece is made as one unit, so that no assembly is needed. Cold-cast porcelain pieces have exceptional detailing and have an excellent surface for painting.

earthenware: a ceramic made of ball clay, kaolin, and pegmatite that is usually glazed and fired, but not vitrified (fired to high temperatures).

feldspar: a type of crystalline mineral.

grotesque: a type of artistic figure developed in the 16th century. The figures are characterized by distorted proportions or incongruous combinations of monstrous or natural forms.

hard-paste porcelain: the hardest porcelain made. The formula for hard-paste porcelain contains feldspar to enhance vitrification and translucence. To achieve this hardness, the porcelain is fired at temperatures as high as 2,642°F.

kaolin: a special clay that is an essential ingredient in porcelain. It is found in quantity in several places around the world. Many of the major porcelain factories are built near these large deposits of kaolin.

kiln: a specially designed oven built to hold carts of ceramic figurines, plates, or other items to be fired or hardened at high temperatures. Most kilns are constructed with openings so that the porcelain can be observed and temperatures controlled to prevent extensive breakage.

majolica: a glazed earthenware that was first made on the Spanish island of Majolica.

Meissen: the first and probably the most famous European porcelain factory, founded in Meissen, Germany, in 1710. The Meissen styles are quite varied and show a mixture of both Western and Eastern influences.

neoclassical art: a revival of classical Greek and Roman forms in art, music, and literature that began during the late 16th century and extended into the 18th century.

pegmatite: a coarse variety of granite.

porcelain: a hard, nonporous ceramic ware made of kaolin, quartz, and feldspar and fired at high temperatures. Porcelain is noted for its translucence and purity. It is sometimes referred to as china.

putto: a cherublike figure appearing as a symbol in Italian Renaissance paintings and sculptures. The plural of *putto* is *putti*. They are often portrayed with wings, and they appear in mythological scenes as companions to the gods.

rococo: a style of art that evolved from the baroque influence in France. The style is characterized by elaborate, profuse designs intended to produce a delicate effect.

Sèvres: the most prestigious porcelain factory in France. The Vincennes Porcelain Factory moved to Sèvres in 1756, where it was known as Vincennes-Sèvres. Later, the company was known simply as Sèvres Porcelain. The early pieces produced by the factory were of the soft-paste variety, but Sèvres was later able to produce a hard paste to rival the porcelains of Germany.

slip: liquid porcelain, usually the thickness of rich cream, which is poured into the molds for porcelain figurines.

soft-paste porcelain: a material resembling hard-paste porcelain but having a softer body. It is mixture of clay and glass fired to around 2,200°F.

Staffordshire: the location in England of one of the most famous porcelain factories. The brightly colored and highly ornate figurines from this factory became so popular and so imitated that the name Staffordshire eventually became the generic term used for all porcelains produced and decorated in this style.

trademark: registered name or identifying symbol impressed or painted on the back or bottom of an item to clearly identify the producer. Producers sometimes make changes in their trademarks, which means that the period during which a piece is made can sometimes be identified.

waste mold: a plaster mold formed around each section of a porcelain piece to be produced. Once the plaster has dried, the mold is opened and the section is removed, leaving the waste mold. The waste mold will then be used to form a case mold or positive form.